the maker

CRAFTING A UNIQUE SPACE

TAMARA MAYNES

WITH TRACY LINES

PHOTOGRAPHY EVE WILSON

ABRAMS | NEW YORK

contents

QUILT LIGHT
TEMPLATE

To the maker, a new project is incredibly alluring. So alluring that we forget the rollercoaster ride that is the creative process and, overcome by desire, leap in wholeheartedly. Head down, surrounded by mess, we work and work and work. As we reach the halfway point of the project, frustration sets in; the concept and our abilities become shrouded in self-doubt, and work is often accompanied by outrageous obscenities. Then, somehow, it's the home stretch and, as if by magic, the fog clears and we enter a state of bliss, until we stand, proud as Punch, holding in all its glory the very thing that showed us both heaven and hell.

Originally seduced by the idea of creating my magnum opus after a lifetime of making, I quickly realized that this project was going to require a whole new level of commitment. When I first started work on *The Maker*, my trusty new assistant Kate by my side, I had no idea quite what I was in for. The creative process was the same as for any project, but this book took every inch of my tenacity, self-confidence, and even temper before it showered me with a feeling of satisfaction more than equal to its demands. (An unexpected bonus is that I now have an extra-extended vocabulary of obscenities!)

Those who follow my work might have expected my first book to be one of cover-to-cover modern craft projects for interiors, but I really wanted to set the stage and allow the reader and/or aspiring maker to think for themself. You see, to be a genuine maker—to earn the badge—means to make from a very honest place, using skills that have been nurtured and honed to bring something into existence that holds your unique fingerprint—your maker's mark. If *The Maker* instills that value in the reader, and that sense of responsibility and camaraderie in the aspiring maker, then I am a happy woman.

I also wanted to take my big, big love of interiors one step further with this book and point out something that, I believe, can be missed as we collect our treasures and decorate our homes with them: the fact that we can only take both of these so far. Making for your space takes it to a level that is much deeper, much more unique, and where, in my opinion, we can really connect.

Happy making,

Tamara.

TO JOHN DENVER, WITH LOVE
chapter one

My work space is an ever-changing treasure trove of inspiration, raw materials, and my own work and that of other makers—such as this wood chair crafted by Melbourne maker Bern Chandley.

Who the hell is John Denver, I hear you ask, and why does he have a chapter dedicated to him? Memories of my very early beginnings as a maker—a time I feel a great connection to and fondness for—will always be accompanied in my head by the sweet folk and country acoustics of this fair-haired American lad. I also borrowed the title of this chapter from the name of the very first collection I launched as a modern craft designer: a re-working of the infamous macramé owl back in 2008. It was both an homage to my beginnings and, unknowingly, a door to my future.

My parents were young when they had me; teenagers, in fact. It was 1971 and by all accounts I was pretty much part of the gang. My memories are of beaches, surfboards, the scorching-hot vinyl seats of our Valiant, an abundance of long sun-bleached hair and gold-tanned skin, and music, music, music. Our house was most unusual and stood out from those that surrounded it because of its uncanny similarity to an igloo. Featured in *The Australian Women's Weekly* in 1952, while it was being built, "La Ronde" was affectionately referred to in the neighborhood as "the roundhouse." In 1976 we swapped the roundhouse for a farmhouse five hours from the coast. With no beach in sight, my parents focused on farming by day and making by night.

The resurgence in craft and making during the 70s not only suited my parents' new lifestyle, but also fostered my beginnings as a maker. While my father's craft of choice was leatherwork, my mother excelled in patchwork and needlepoint and went on frequent adventures, mastering and eventually selling and teaching an abundance of crafts. There was always something being made in our home: more often than not a tray of enameled jewelry would need to come out of the oven before dinner could go in, or a half-stitched quilt had to be removed from the kitchen table before we could eat.

Influenced by my parents, I experimented with different crafts, challenging my ability with the assistance of a seemingly natural affinity. It is the memories of my mother's store, Country Road Craft Supplies (named after a song by her musical love of the time: you guessed it—John Denver), that holds my personal connection to macramé and that very first collection. The afternoons I spent at the shop after school were heavenly and (if I wasn't at the convenience store next door, having my appetite spoiled by the beehived shopkeeper) I was more than content to marvel at the multitude of colored wooden beads, metal rings, and huge skeins of macramé yarns on display.

As a teenager I was incredibly interested in expressing my creativity through clothing. Despite living on a farm on the outskirts of a country town that had absolutely zero interest in fashion, I managed to do this by using my passion and skill for sewing to make or rework everything I wore. By now it was the 1980s and I was conjuring a weird fusion of Molly Ringwald in *Pretty in Pink* and Madonna in *Desperately Seeking Susan*. This meant searching through the pattern books at the local fabric store in search of something to alter, or using my country girl charm to worm my way into the backrooms and unexplored treasures of the two local, second-hand clothing shops. At the very least I would make my own buttons from oven-bake clay or change the hem of a dress, so, in some way, shape, or form, there was a new outfit, most often outside the box, made every week. Certain people in my life fostered this expression, not least my mother, whom I could always count on to put some of the more narrow-minded country folk in their place on my behalf.

While wearing my latest creations to round up sheep in the dusty paddocks, I dreamed with fervor of moving to the city and becoming the junior fashion editor at *Dolly* magazine. But leaving home at seventeen and arriving in Sydney shortly afterwards, I quickly realized there were at least a thousand girls with the same idea and, although I pursued my hope of working in fashion magazines for a number of years, even briefly in London, I never made it beyond internships and test shoots. I had a ball and delved passionately and successfully into many aspects of the fashion world—predominantly design, production, and brand creation—but gaining full access to any of the publications was one place my country girl charm couldn't get me.

I'd never given much thought to working with interiors. Although I'd always been very aware of how I wanted my space to look and extremely involved in making it unique, it wasn't until I started to feel disillusioned with the fashion industry that my blinders were removed. Being introduced to *Elle Decoration UK* magazine by a visual merchandising colleague in the early 90s blew my mind. I wanted to explode after reading it and taking in the imagery for the first time. I still look forward to it every month, and add each issue to my ever-growing collection that now spans twenty years. The odd *Vogue* or *Harper's Bazaar* gets a look in now and then, but the sparkle I once saw in fashion is gone.

Things moved ahead quickly and organically for me once I discovered interiors. At first I focused on making limited edition and custom homewares for boutique stores and interior decorators; this then evolved into making props for interior stylists and fabric showrooms, which then turned into developing specialized products for interior retailers.

I have been sewing ever since I can remember. I love it. LOVE it. This old girl has been with me for over a decade and our relationship is one of mutual respect. She's as heavy as a small car and a total bitch to move, but I would drag her out of a burning building if it ever came down to it!

I was drawing on the making skills I'd developed while growing up, including my father's love of leatherwork, which featured heavily in my custom pieces. On one particular trip back to the farm, I brazenly made off with his original leatherwork tools, claiming them as my own. I still have a small selection of this kit that manages to transport me effortlessly back to the farmhouse table whenever I revisit leatherwork.

Something happened when my husband and I decided, in our late thirties after twenty years in Sydney, that we needed a country hiatus. Our little refresher pause came in the form of a wisteria-covered cottage complete with fireplace and converted barn kitchen, and it was here that everything changed for me as a maker. Stripped of the excessive visual noise of the city I slipped into self-awareness. Very quickly, and certainly without trying, I was able to connect to what really resonated with me. Going with the flow, I decided that I would redesign the macramé owl of my childhood. Who knows whether it was the country air fooling me back into my youth or the pile of my mother's treasured craft books in my possession, but I was incredibly inspired. Considering macramé had died an ugly death after the 70s I had no idea if the world was ready to embrace a modern version of the owl, let alone the craft itself. Yet here we are some seven years later and not only did the world embrace my owl and the resurgence of macramé, but I was catapulted headfirst into a new way of seeing my making practice and sharing my output.

My online store, The Six Week Boutique, certainly wasn't my first foray into selling my wares but it was my first online, and it was perfect, considering my geographical isolation. It was very early days for the small group of independent makers who, like me, were focused on introducing modern craft for interiors, particularly those setting up online. Its immediate success was due to a somewhat unexpectedly hungry audience and a very lucky case of good timing. Being featured on then relatively new blogs, such as The Design Files, Design★ Sponge, and Apartment Therapy, I couldn't knot fast enough to keep up with demand. When I added modern versions of cross-stitch kits, inspired by my trouser-wearing motorcycle-riding great grandmother, things got even crazier. I began to receive requests to teach others to make and to speak about modern craft to audiences and interviewers, and eventually I took on the project design and production of modern DIY for *Inside Out* magazine's "Why Don't You?" page. After adding the role of Craft Editor for independent magazine *SoHi* to my expanding career, I watched as my skill as a maker, understanding as a designer, and ever-increasing affection for interiors grew into the perfect love triangle.

Being involved in the journeys of other aspiring makers through the sharing of my own output made me realize just how collective yet unique making is. From the popularity of a modern craft DIY project in a much-loved interior magazine, to witnessing a room full of people learn the same basic skills yet produce something wonderfully individual, it became clear that making brings us together while allowing us to be ourselves. Taking this fundamental idea and applying it to the creation of a space, the making of a home, made perfect sense, and still does.

Today, I stand by this awareness, employing it as the backbone of my work as both maker and designer, creative director and stylist, teacher and mentor. Intertwined on a daily basis, these aspects all support and encourage each other but when, on occasion, I feel I can't breathe, I'm very clear it's the maker in me that needs prioritizing. Spending quality time with raw materials and technique, alone in the quiet possibility of collaboration, is pure freedom and when I'm most able to feel content and energized by the fellowship I share with other makers.

"Color is one of my biggest drivers as a maker; I have never been scared of it. Although, when I teach others to make, it's always in monochrome so the aspiring maker can focus on learning technique and skill. Keeping color out of the picture allows you to linger in the craft and not get caught up purely in aesthetics or end results."

"

My most precious tools are my hands. Yes, they are slightly on the calloused side from a lifetime of making, but they can stitch, shape, build, and craft their way into or out of pretty much anything.

"

THE MAKER'S MARK
chapter two

Making is such a personal experience. For me it's when I am most grounded and, while I remain incredibly present, what I am making is in a state of unfolding with its sights set on the future. As my hands work and mind rests, a tangible form takes shape and begins a life of its own. It's both a humble and powerful feeling, knowing your technique intimately, dancing quietly with a raw material, guiding it to become something more, and knowing when to allow it to lead. Standing back to admire its finished form, you can't help but feel you have contributed something meaningful —that you have left your mark.

Whatever shape or form the mark is made in, the practice of each individual maker is usually fueled by a combination of elements. In my case, I have a lingering fascination with the past. Maybe it's not so much a fascination as a sense of nostalgia; either way, I feel compelled to see it exist fresh-faced in the present and able to stand tall in the years to come. Despite many traditional making practices being lost through the centuries or modernized by technology, I love that makers today, whether they realize it or not, are essentially carrying on the legacy of those who made before them. Of course, every maker's mark is theirs alone, but the foundations of the modern maker are rooted in history. As a maker myself, this thought provokes in me a true sense of camaraderie – of belonging to something significant.

The differences between us modern makers and our medieval comrades are substantial but on a fundamental level we couldn't be more connected. Making, when embraced and nurtured, is like winning the lottery of self-fulfillment. The delight in bringing something beautiful into existence with your bare hands is as rewarding today as I'm sure it was hundreds, if not thousands, of years ago.

In an added layer of sentimentality, I also have a tendency to identify more with the makers of the past who crafted pieces specifically for their homes and the spaces of others. From rickety three-legged wooden stools and rustic tin dinner plates shaped by humble makers, to intricately carved four-poster beds and finely built porcelain tea sets formed by master craftsmen, I cannot help but feel inspired and in awe of past makers who forged the way, intent on bringing comfort, beauty, and individuality to where and how they lived.

generations of cleverness

Humans have been makers since the beginning of time. And, in light of the early troubleshooting we needed in order to simply eat, sleep, and protect ourselves from the elements, we were also incredible designers. Granted, the output of those early makers—predominantly stone tools, weapons, and utensils—is seemingly naïve. On closer inspection, however, the techniques formed in response to available materials illustrate just how proficient we were with our hands right from the get-go. Let's face it: makers are a bunch of impressively clever folks.

As time passed, our skill, along with our maker's eye, developed and we went from making for survival, to considering pleasure, expressing status, and applying comfort. In terms of creating a home, when early makers began to discover and appreciate the value of aesthetics, making took on a whole new meaning and was expressed through the introduction of surface

William Morris, 1834–96, was the founder of the British Arts and Crafts Movement and a passionate advocate for the makers' output following the Industrial Revolution.

decoration, precious materials, and intricate forms. As our capabilities progressed, so too did the ease with which our daily tasks could be performed, leaving some of us with time in the day to make for enjoyment.

Now picture this. . . it's the Middle Ages and making, which until now has been a free-for-all, becomes controlled by the individual guilds that are formed to represent every handicraft within all towns and cities. Due to their geographical scattering, country folk are exempt and remain as entrepreneurs trading under the term "cottage industry." But city dwellers across Europe are now required to operate under guild regulations. Monopolistic in nature, the guilds are a ticket to riches for those who determine the laws and have the power to grant who makes what, where, for whom, and for what price. The makers have these laws imposed upon them and, well, they are somewhat bummed. The learning maker now faces years as a beginner apprentice, followed by many more years as a middle-level journeyman, before producing a masterpiece that will hopefully gain him the title of Master Craftsman, full admission to the guild, and permission to trade. Focusing on the positive, it is certainly a favorable move in the creation of standards for craftsmanship.

Fast forward to the late 1700s as the Industrial Revolution swings into action. Machines are taking over the making of everything we need. Like collapsing lines of dominoes, makers are quickly made superfluous, guilds start to fold, and our household furniture and objects become aesthetically utilitarian. It seems the value of craftsmanship and the maker will be lost, until the heroic form of an English architect arrives to save the day. Enter, in 1860-ish, William Morris, a man who desperately loves the makers' output and despises what the Industrial Revolution has done to craftsmanship. In an effort to change attitudes in Britain he sets about reviving traditional crafts and production methods by establishing Morris & Co, a super-hip decorative arts firm. Making and selling highly decorative tapestries, wallpaper, fabric, furniture, and stained-glass windows, Morris's efforts result in a crusade that is labeled the Arts and Crafts Movement. His statement "Have nothing in your house that you do not know to be useful, or believe to be beautiful," unknowingly heralds the arrival of the makers' liberator: modernism, in which utility is as important as beauty. While Morris does an awesome job of bringing attention back to the maker and the unique decorating of a space, the price of craftsmanship still has unbeatable competition in the form of affordable machine-made goods. Alas, it seems as if things can only be produced one way or the other.

Something has got to give and indeed it does, half a century later in 1919 at the hands of another architect, Walter Gropius. This innovative thinker cleverly introduces a modern "less is more" approach to design. A fan of Morris, Gropius opens a school in Germany named *Staatliches Bauhaus*. It becomes known simply as Bauhaus —the name translates to "house of building"—but strangely its teachings are not focused on architecture, but rather the combining of craft with fine arts, which has traditionally been a bit of a no-no. Bauhaus students are taught to look at household objects with a fresh eye, merging craft with technology. The Bauhaus message that form should always follow function, that design should be reduced to its most essential elements, and that there is a way to make peace between mass production and craftsmanship produces furniture such as a set of minimalist nesting tables crafted from solid oak and lacquered acrylic glass. The Bauhaus teachings become an influential design movement and, although the school is closed down in 1933 by the Nazi government, many of its faculty emigrate to the USA and continue to spread and practice its ideologies. Influencing the output of icons such as Charles and Ray Eames, for example, the Bauhaus philosophies continue to provide makers with a solid foundation on which to use good design, craft, and technology to make their output unique and affordable.

Historian I am not, as you can now attest, but this tale of guilds, revolution, and modernism illustrates that we modern makers are a lucky bunch—those who came before have done all the groundwork, leaving us armed with incredible raw materials, technologically advanced tools, and an awareness of good design and technique.

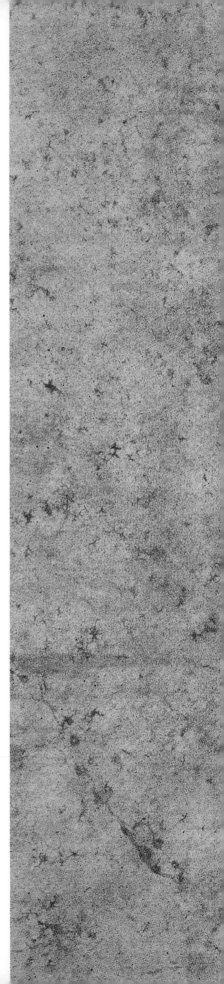

*Walter Gropius, 1883–1969, was the
force behind the Bauhaus teachings,
responsible for the fine marriage
of craftsmanship and technology
applied in modernism.*

developing a maker's eye

Makers have a certain way of looking at the objects around them: a tendency to study them visually, exploring and deconstructing until they make sense, until it's understood how the object was formed and from what, stopping only when a connection is formed to the hand that made it. Curious creatures when it comes to the tangible, makers are like chefs who instinctively pinpoint ingredients with their tastebuds while eating another's food. Over time a maker's eye is developed unknowingly, quietly adding to their understanding of techniques, materials, and design. But how do we even know what craft is the right one for us, or which raw material we will have the deepest connection to? Before you can develop your eye you need to develop a level of self-awareness.

Obviously the modern maker of yore both have inspirational driving forces—things that push them to choose a particular craft or practice—but what they might not have in common is what those forces are. For example, the driving force of early makers was survival, while medieval makers added comfort, pleasure, and status. Modern makers on the other hand are downright spoiled in this department and have the freedom and luxury to be driven by their deepest, most heartfelt inspirations. The more you allow yourself to be aware of everything, from your core values and personality traits, what inspires and challenges you as an individual, to what colors, textures, and shapes resonate with you, the more a craft, or at the very least a category, will speak to you.

Let's face it, as with anything, to have an authentic experience you need to know what floats your boat. Walk in nature, visit exhibitions, watch films, fill sketch books: do whatever you need to find some space to know yourself inside and out.

The second key to developing a maker's eye is nurturing skill. Discovering your craft is only the beginning and, just like the medieval makers operating under guild laws, you must give yourself time to bond with your material and technique, discover its strengths and weaknesses, and experiment to achieve mastery. Finding a good teacher and affording yourself time to learn, develop, and explore all make a great difference to the maturing of the maker's eye, and therefore the authenticity of their output. Teaching yourself isn't a bad thing of course—a lack of formal training and impressing of rules has offered many a maker (myself included) the freedom to develop their eye unfettered; just don't let this option hinder the nurturing of real skill. Craftsmanship, or skill, is what gives you power as a maker. It lets you trust that your hands will work diligently to form what you see in your mind and feel in your bones.

You can spot a maker by their tenacity, worker's hands, overwhelming need to create, and tendency to collect making paraphernalia. Their output, however, is a different matter completely. Despite our standout traits as a collective, we are all incredibly unique, so I certainly don't intend to pigeonhole the modern maker, but there do seem to be distinctive maker "types." Distinguishable by their output, the eyes of these makers have been developed by shared drivers and skills. There are many different types of makers, but three examples I am personally drawn to are the innovative modernist, the foraging naturalist, and the imaginative revivalist. There are also rebel makers who blur the lines, merging or even transcending type to stand alone.

Whether the maker is driven by advances in technology, a connection to nature, the desire to give vintage a second go, or something else entirely, it is always a combination of inspiration, individuality, and skill that determines the maker's mark.

THE MODERNIST

is a risk taker who has his or her finger on the pulse, is a pioneer in the development and use of raw materials and techniques, lives for innovation, sees things in terms of sustainability, pushes the envelope, and breaks new ground.

THE NATURALIST

is a gentle soul, has an overwhelming connection to the seasons, is privy to the source of raw materials, loves to forage, sees his or her output as an extension of nature, plays with organic form, and is guaranteed to make imperfection desirable.

THE REVIVALIST

is imaginative, has a knack for taking dated materials and techniques to a fresh place, is a big fan of redesign, loves to shake things up, sees new in the old, plays with merging eras, and is determined to rewrite the rules.

beyond decorating

Making gives you the incredible ability via your hands to create a space that is yours on a very personal level. The same could be said for the treasures you collect for your home and the way you style them, but the act of actually having created those treasures takes the space to a deeper level; it goes beyond collecting, beyond decorating. There is incredible soul in a kitchen whose table was built by the person eating at it, or whose bed is made warm with a quilt stitched by the person sleeping under it.

I am a renter, and being the homebody I am, I never quite feel secure knowing that at any time I could be instructed to move on. Considering Australian renters are unable to paint walls or make other cosmetic changes, the thing that has saved me is making. The fact that I live in a space that doesn't belong to me is blurred by the energy of the pieces that fill it, in particular the pieces I have made. I connect so deeply with them that no matter what wall they hang on, or corner they light, I am home.

I'm not suggesting that you attempt to master all crafts and fill every room in your home with your own harvest, never to buy a pre-made item again. It's not about cutting yourself off from enjoying the output of other makers, the beauty of inherited or found pieces, or even the convenience of mass-produced items. It's about injecting a very intimate part of yourself into the mix and quite literally "making" your space yours.

The following chapters feature many of my favorite making practices, the output and words of admired makers, inspiration, and hard information on taking the common aspects of any interior such as wall art, objects, textiles, ceramics, lighting, and furniture to a deeper level via making. Each chapter closes with an introductory project directed at aspiring makers as further encouragement. Definitely not to be considered as DIY, these projects are focused and simple in purpose, in an effort to allow you to think for yourself, to make from feeling, with only the fundamentals to guide you.

WHAT TO EXPLORE
chapter three

appliqué

Appliqué, meaning "applied," is the adhering of ornament to a surface for decoration. It is most commonly used in the making of textiles, where it is achieved by stitching independent fabric pieces to a backing cloth to form a pattern or design, and is also seen in ceramic work. Appliqué is not always focused on independently: it often forms part of a broader textile practice, such as quilting, or is used in general sewing projects. Appliqué is slow, steady work and requires perfection and patience, particularly when creating intricate patterns.

basketry

Basketry is a beautiful craft whose process, depending on your material source, can begin well before any actual weaving takes place. Foraging for materials found in nature, such as willow along riverbanks, grasses, or even the collection of humble twigs, adds to the organic quality of basketry. So does the time-consuming preparation of materials, both found and bought, such as rattan cane. Once prepared, materials are woven using a variety of techniques: coiling, plaiting, twining, and wickerwork (when the material is woven in and around a stiff frame). As well as enjoying a deep connection to nature, the basket maker has good opportunity to be a sustainable maker.

ceramics

At its core there is something magical about making ceramics: the moment your hands meet the raw material of this practice you will be won over. Don't let this passion fool you, though: there is real skill involved in making ceramics, and achieving even the simplest of forms requires technique and perseverance. Ceramics are predominantly either hand-built (meaning the clay is rolled out and cut to shape before being joined) or wheel-thrown (forms are made by rotation on a potter's wheel). Both techniques have their individual variances. Of the two, hand-building is a considerably more straightforward technique than wheel throwing, and requires less learned skill. The ceramics project on page 170 is a good introduction to working with clay.

chair caning

The caning, or weaving, of chair seats and/or backs is not difficult, but takes time and patience to perfect. The repetitive practice of chair cane (the outer bark of rattan) being woven into a lattice pattern is often seen in classic Thonet bentwood chairs. Other materials and techniques used to weave chair seats are Shaker tape (fabric tape is woven in a checkerboard pattern on Shaker-style chairs) and Danish- or paper-cord, in which twisted brown kraft paper cord is typically woven into four triangles whose points meet in the center, as seen in many mid-century chairs such as Hans Wegner's Wishbone.

embroidery

Embroidery is entirely addictive: the house could be falling down and the embroiderer might not even notice! This type of hand-stitching is used in the embellishment of fabric, although it has been known to adorn other base materials, such as paper and wood. Embroidery is another form of fabric surface decoration and employs a variety of stitches in textured yarns to create patterns or designs. This is a craft that belies its age: the stitches used in embroidery today are the same as those in the earliest samples from the third century BC.

fabric dyeing & printing

Embellishing fabric is a very different practice than producing fabric, and offers an experimental experience to the textile maker. Fabric dyeing and printing can use "resist" techniques to block some areas of fabric to the paint or dye and allow it to color other areas, forming a pattern or design. Popular resist techniques are shibori, in which fabric is folded, stitched, twisted, and compressed with rubber bands or thread, often around small pieces of wood and poles, before being immersed in a dye bath, and screen- or block-printing, in which a design in paint or dye is transferred onto fabric via a silkscreen or stamp.

felting

Felting is an experimental craft based on the fact that fibers bind to each other when they are tangled or agitated. Fibers that can be felted successfully are those covered in tiny scales which assist the binding process; these include sheep's wool, mohair or cashmere from goats, and angora from rabbits. The felter can use two techniques: dry (or needle) felting and wet felting. Dry felting forms a dense mass that is suited to making objects. Wet felting, which uses water and agitation to encourage the fibers to bind, forms a dense fabric that lends itself to the creation of larger two-dimensional pieces such as wall hangings. It is not uncommon for felters to also have a keen interest and involvement in the production of their raw material.

glass blowing

Glass blowing is all about air inflation and its ability to expand molten (melted) glass. Representing a deeper understanding of the properties of glass, it was invented during the first century BC at the height of the Roman Empire, which embraced this new technology. The art of glass blowing comprises both free-blowing, when the glass blower uses short puffs of air to inflate a molten blob at the end of a pipe before working it into shape using rotation and other controlled moves, and mold-blowing, when the molten glass is still placed on the end of a pipe but is inflated directly into a mold to form its shape. Glass blowing is used to form vessels and lighting and involves learned skill and patience, not to mention a good set of lungs.

knitting

One of the most widespread and irresistible of the textile and fiber crafts, knitting is essentially a fabric production method in which stitches are created by looping yarn in consecutive rows using a pair of knitting needles. Fabric outcome in terms of weight, texture, and character is dependent on a combination of needle size, tension, yarn, and stitch type and can be used for textile pieces such as throws, cushions, furniture, and lighting. Ultra-fine work is used for lampshades, while the chunkiest throws are achieved using giant needles and thick yarn. Knitters' fingers work incredibly swiftly and, due to the slow-forming nature of their work, they must often summon bucketloads of resolve. In return they are rewarded with a lovely, meditative making experience.

leaded glasswork

This glasswork technique was first used to make stained glass or leadlight windows, but during the nineteenth century leaded, or "came," glasswork moved into three-dimensional forms such as sculpture, terrariums, and lighting. Two-dimensional leaded glasswork assembles pieces of cut glass with "cames," metal divider strips, usually made of lead or zinc, which join the glass pieces, provide the metal to be soldered, and form the decorative lines within the glasswork. In three-dimensional work, the copper-foil and solder method, or "Tiffany method," is used. Developed by the son of the Tiffany & Co. founder, this method made possible a level of detail that was previously unknown by drawing on the flexibility and strength of copper to create more intricate and lightweight pieces.

leatherwork

Leatherwork is the crafting of objects, textiles, lighting, and furniture from animal skin that has been processed into leather. The practice requires skill and physicality; it also requires much experimentation to master. Leatherwork often involves not only shaping but also surface decoration. Shaping can be done by cutting and hand-sewing, or by a technique known as *cuir bouilli* (literally: boiled leather) in which the leather is soaked in hot water until pliable, then either shaped by hand or with the use of a mold until it dries and becomes very stiff. Embellishment can be achieved by various carving, stamping, dyeing, or painting techniques.

macramé

Part of my own ongoing making practice, macramé is essentially the repetitive knotting of rope to form an intertwined pattern. Macramé is highly decorative and revolves around one central material: rope, and lots of it. Rope is usually mounted onto a strong rod or ring for large-scale projects and often worked from the height of a ladder. Used predominantly for making wall art, macramé can also be seen in lighting and furniture. This highly interpretive craft relies on the knowledge of a catalog of various knots. It is physically demanding and its success is dependent on preparation, attention to detail, and regular chiropractor visits to relieve upper body tension—trust me!

metalwork

Metalwork is a broad term and is often associated with sculpture, lighting, kitchenware, and furniture making. There are many processes used to work metal and they can be categorized into three main areas: forming (for example, forging hot metal and spinning cold metal into vessels and lighting); cutting; and joining (of which the two most common examples are welding and soldering). Joining is possibly the most achievable for aspiring makers and requires (as does any type of metalworking) a fastidious approach, technical knowledge of materials, commitment to safe practices and working conditions, and fine motor skills. The wall-hanging project on page 80 is a good introduction to working with metal.

papercraft

It is often hard to believe that such incredible work— wall art, objects, lighting—can be made from an everyday material like paper. Using a variety of techniques such as modeling and sculpting (in which paper is cut, glued, and ultimately reworked into a three-dimensional form), cutting (to create textured flat surfaces), and origami (folding paper into three-dimensional forms), paper practice has the ability to create things that are far from "everyday." Another paper technique, albeit a little different, rather messy and slow working, is papier-mâché. This process begins with a lightweight base (often cardboard) upon which many layers of torn paper are pasted to build a form. The form can be sanded, drilled, and painted once it has dried hard.

quilting & patchwork

Quilting is a sewing technique used predominantly in the making of quilts (hence the name!). The process involves joining layers of material, typically three: a decorative top layer; a middle layer of batting or other insulating material; and a plain backing fabric. This results in a bulkier material. Quilting employs a running, or straight, stitch that can be sewn by hand with a needle and thread or with a sewing machine. Patchwork is the stitching together of small pieces of contrasting fabrics to form a pattern or design (called a block) and is traditionally used to form the top layer of a quilt. Both machine- and hand-quilters will need to summon accuracy, resolve, and patience to complete a quality quilt.

rug hooking

Floor rugs are a staple in every space and are often produced by machine for affordability. When they are made using techniques such as hand-knotting—as in intricate Persian rugs—these pieces can take up to a year to craft. The labor involved, coupled with the level of quality this brings, produces rugs of heirloom standard which are highly priced. A couple of more achievable methods of rug making are called hooking and latch-hooking and can produce a patterned, sturdy, and heavily textured floor covering in a much shorter time. During the repetitive hooking process, loops of yarn are pulled through a rigid woven base by two different techniques, using the appropriate version of a specialized, crochet-like hook tool. Warning: patience is essential!

sculpture

Sculpture is essentially the making of any two- or three-dimensional representative or abstract form. The shaping techniques vary according to the raw materials being used, for example: the sculpting of a pair of ice skates using paper that is cut, glued, and reworked into a 3D form; the formation of a plaster bust using a mold; or a collection of twigs and branches or welded steel rods that has been constructed into abstract wall art. Because the practice of sculpture spans so many methods and materials, the personal level of skill required of the individual maker varies greatly.

shade making

Making shades for lighting could be seen as a flippant craft, but it is one that is open to serious interpretation. The diffusing of light in a space can be transformative and with this in mind, the maker should consider both form and function. Luckily, the list of techniques employed —leaded glasswork, basketry, ceramics, macramé, leatherwork, and metalwork—can all afford the shade maker the leverage to do this successfully. Typical shade-making practice involves the construction and covering of a metal rod frame in fabric. Depending on the shape of the frame, this can take substantial technical, pattern-making, and sewing skills to perfect.

tapestry weaving

This experimental fiber art is as addictive as any other in the textiles category and its creations are often at their best gracing a space as wall art. Tapestry weaving is practiced on a weaving loom; it is different from the production of cloth on a loom in that a design is formed by weaving the weft thread over the warp, covering the warp completely (most woven cloth shows both the warp and weft threads). The early days of any weaving practice require patience as the process is a slow one, but with skill will come speed. See the project on page 140 for an introduction to tapestry weaving.

upholstery

I have seen many an aspiring maker take on an upholstery project only to quickly discover what hard work is required. Physical and labor-intensive, upholstery is a commitment. However, being aware of your skill level and starting with a project that is appropriate to this will make the process enjoyable. Depending on the furniture being upholstered, the process of this craft often begins with the addition of a spring system to a (usually) wood frame, followed by the construction and/or renovation of cushions and padding and, finally, the covering of these with fabric or leather, which might involve sewing or the use of specialized upholstery hammers and nails.

willow bending

Willow bending is the nature-loving furniture maker's dream come true. First, a frame is made up of the thicker parts of willow branches, called rods. Switches, the thinner and more pliable ends of the willow branch, are then bent and woven into this frame. Bending willow to make furniture requires carpentry skills and a connection to and understanding of working with materials found in nature. Some craft practices have a strong association with the sourcing of their materials and willow bending is a good example of this. Preparation usually entails the selection and collection of willow from its natural riverside habitat, followed by lengthy periods of drying out of the rods and switches, followed by soaking prior to bending.

wirework

Wirework is an uncomplicated and relatively simple craft, using straightforward materials and tools, but it can be harder than it looks. Used in lighting, wall art, and the sculpture of objects, wirework is all about technique. These techniques are based on the use of various pliers to form curves, straighten, twist, and cut. The rest is up to the maker's hands and imagination. See the project on page 80 for a good introduction to sculpting with wire.

woodwork

Woodwork is an inclusive term that covers a variety of crafts focusing on wood as their core material. Makers working with wood can practice techniques that fall into many different categories. Carving can be done by hand for vessels or small objects, or with the use of a chainsaw for furniture. Turning is the shaping of wood as it rotates on a lathe. Furniture and cabinet making require the cutting and joining of wood to form larger pieces. The woodworker can also focus on surface decoration such as pyrography, in which a design is burned into wood, and marquetry, in which wood veneer is cut out and rejoined to form thin, decorative panels which are stuck to the face of a furniture carcass. The woodworker requires dexterity and a good understanding of the tools and materials used. The lighting project on page 200 is a good introduction to woodwork, while the project on page 232 gives an introduction to a combination of marquetry and parquetry.

WALL ART
chapter four

Makers focusing on wall art seem to have a very experimental attitude toward their craft. Perhaps this hails from the combination of an entire wall as a blank canvas and minimal need for function. Really, it's all about form, and form can come in any size, shape, or material and from any inspiration.

One form I will never forget is a large piece of wall art my mother made when she was in her mid-twenties: a tiger, painted in perfect detail in Hobbytex★ onto a solid black velvet surface, that crouched majestically above our living room sofa. Keeping in mind that it was the 1970s and black velvet and Hobbytex were considered incredibly fabulous, it was through this piece that my mother managed to express the skill of her hand and, unintentionally, the youth and vitality of our family and home. At the time, my young maker's eye was developing and our velvet tiger fascinated me. The way its blended stripes fell gently away into the raised surface of the velvet and the touches of gold in its coat, which sparkled ever so slightly through the fibers, was mesmerizing. Today, some 36 years on, while Hobbytex and black velvet are no longer considered incredibly fabulous, my feelings for that tiger still linger. I remain acutely aware of where the furniture was placed and of the gifted and inherited objects in that room, and the tiger gives it all a residual sense of place.

The following pages feature a collection of wall art that has been felted, cut, knotted, stitched, welded, sculpted, painted, or glued by many makers' hands—some by my own and others by makers whose work I am inspired by. Shown styled within different spaces and settings, they illustrate the many facets of wall art, the self-expression it offers, and the ability it has to go beyond decorating. They should also serve as inspiration for your own unique wall art pieces and, ultimately, space.

★ *Hobbytex is a trademarked fabric paint of paste-like consistency, contained in a soft metal tube and fed with gentle pressure through a specialized nib.*

Circular macramé wall hanging, using polypropylene rope and polished copper hardware / Tamara Maynes

As I mastered the technique of macramé
it felt natural to experiment with design
and see where the knots could take
me. I love that I managed to bring this
technique out of the era it's associated
with and move it forward.

TAMARA MAYNES

"
I started felting because someone gave me seven bags of alpaca fleece! Making felt is elemental and primitive: the combination of only nature's intelligent design and my elbow grease. I get into a rhythm. I need a whole day. I need to be alone. I am completely absorbed.
"

HARRIET GOODALL, FIBER ARTIST & BASKET MAKER
(ROBERTSON, AUSTRALIA)

Modern tribal mask, using papier-mâché layer
built over plywood frame / Tamara Maynes &
Machine-sewn and hand-painted coiled cotton
rope vessels / Gemma Patford Legge

"
When I make, I zone out. I'm meditative. I listen to audio books. I am covered in paint. I tangle the cat up with rope. I experiment.
"

GEMMA PATFORD LEGGE, MAKER
(MELBOURNE, AUSTRALIA)

> **"**
>
> # No matter how many times I move and how many different walls I hang my papier-mâché mask on, seeing it staring back always makes me feel I'm home.
>
> **"**

TAMARA MAYNES

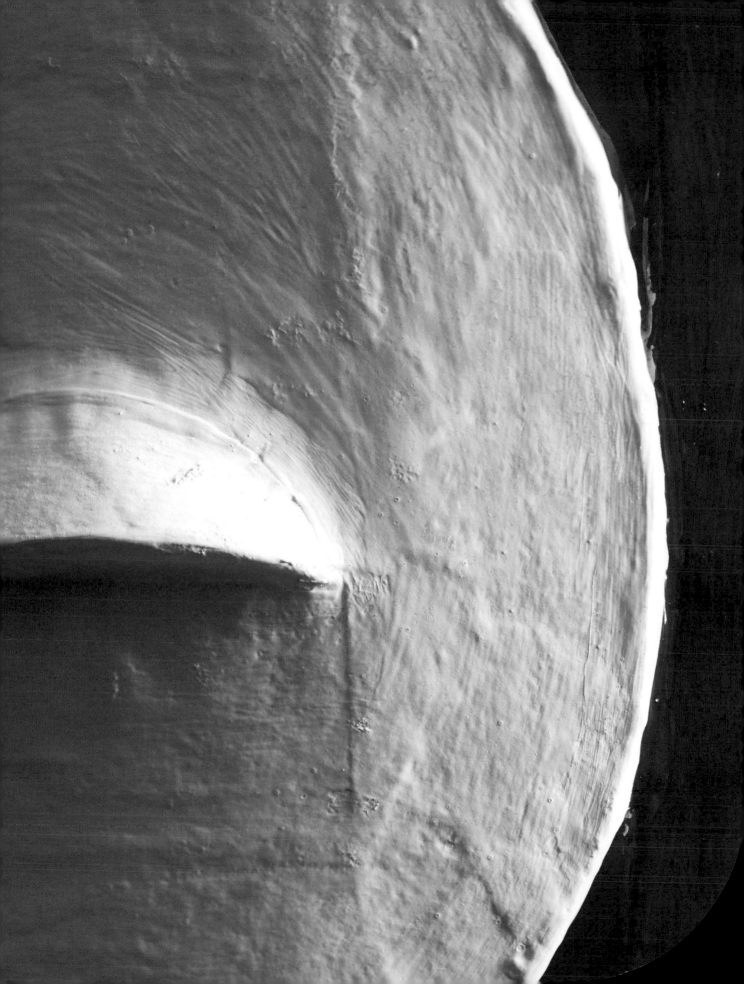

Q&A

Maker to Maker with...

Kate Keara Pelen, fine artist

(London, UK)

TM: Kate, what materials do you use?
KKP: These pieces are embroidered using cotton and synthetic threads on linen cotton.

TM: How did you get into embroidery?
KKP: A few years ago I was working on a piece for a church interior. I became fascinated by the modest, unsung tradition of embroidered hassocks and it took off from there.

TM: You are also an abstract painter, which is such a different practice from embroidery. What draws you to these two extremes?
KKP: Working with needle and thread, slowly and steadily creating tactile compositions, provides me with an interesting counterpoint to the energy and speed of abstract painting. In contrast to painting, embroidery helps to still my sometimes restless mind.

TM: Can you describe your process?
KKP: My embroidery is always abstract and derived from what I notice and appreciate, rather than identifiable scenes or objects that I wish to represent. I start with a clutch of colors and a particular piece of fabric to stitch onto, but the rest is entirely improvised. The first few stitches tend to determine the direction of the piece; although I try not to think about an end point and rather just explore, leaving my hands to work things out as they go along.

TM: Where do you make?
KKP: I am at my best working in a fairly organized and tidy space, at a large table surrounded by threads arranged by color.

TM: What does embroidery bring to a space?
KKP: It brings a surface that is, curiously, also an object.

TM: Any advice for aspiring embroiderers?
KKP: Be open to inspiration from everywhere. It could be the shape or color of a vegetable at the market, the pattern on a wall, or a piece of music that conjures up images in your mind.

"I WORK QUICKLY AND INTUITIVELY;
I'M ABSORBED BY THE MOMENT.
I WORK ALONE, BUT THERE IS A
CONSTANT INTERNAL DIALOGUE –
IDEAS POPPING, HANDS
TRYING TO KEEP UP."

DION HORSTMANS, METAL SCULPTOR & ARTIST
(SYDNEY, AUSTRALIA)

"The cycles of nature and beauty in
organic materials are the source of
my creativity. These allow me to draw
inspiration from their form and
create something truly unique."

WONA BAE, FLORIST & STICK SCULPTOR
(MELBOURNE, AUSTRALIA)

"Making has no rules, no restrictions. It's whatever you want it to be. The beauty of working with paper is that you can change it from something very basic to something quite extraordinary. A simple fold can create a new perspective."

MARSHA GOLEMAC, STYLIST, ART DIRECTOR, & PAPER ARTIST
(MELBOURNE, AUSTRALIA)

Uashmama washable paper, layered and cut wall hanging, hung on dowel rod / Marsha Golemac

"A MAKER'S KNOWLEDGE AND UNDERSTANDING OF THEIR MATERIALS AND PROCESSES IS SOMETHING VERY INTIMATE AND UNIQUE. IT'S GOOD TO WORK WITH ONE TECHNIQUE OVER A NUMBER OF YEARS: YOU CAN REALLY PUSH AND EXPLORE ITS BOUNDARIES."

THE FORTYNINE STUDIO COLLECTIVE OF DESIGNERS & MAKERS
(SYDNEY, AUSTRALIA)

"I ENJOY THE SLOW, TEDIOUS PARTS OF MY MAKING PRACTICE AS MUCH AS THE EXCITING BITS. IT MAKES ALL THE DIFFERENCE, BECAUSE METALWORK IS SLOW AND HARD."

ANNA VARENDORFF, JEWELER & SCULPTOR
(MELBOURNE, AUSTRALIA)

"IN MY MIND ARE STAMPED FROM PREVIOUS TEACHERS: 'EMBRACE THE WOBBLE,' AND 'TEST, TEST, TEST!'"

MICHELE QUAN, CERAMIC SCULPTOR
(NEW YORK, USA)

a word on...
CRAFTSMANSHIP

I fear craftsmanship can be a little taken for granted in our fast-paced world and for that reason I love to advocate its importance. Ultimately, craftsmanship is the skill a maker possesses, one that is established over time and based on strong technique, good design, and a genuine understanding of their raw materials. You may not know the maker, but, if they have mastered their craft, their craftsmanship will be visible and, without sounding too dramatic, have the ability to astound. Reaching that level of mastery in your chosen craft means practicing patience, conjuring commitment, and coming from a place of passion. Anyone with a spare afternoon can whip up something handmade, but a true maker will obsess over every small detail, research the perfect material, and take the utmost care and pride in making something worthy of the title.

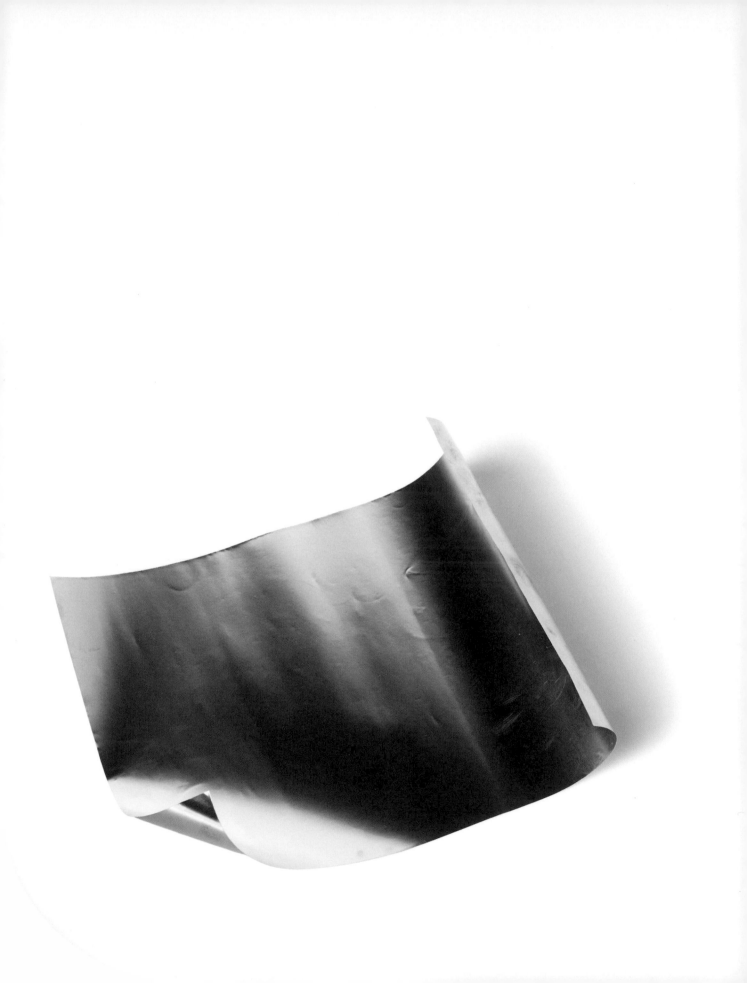

PROJECT Nº1

metalwork wall hanging

The template on the following pages is a guide only and not to scale. A complete ready-to-print template and layout guide can be found at www.tamaramaynes.com.

This project is a great introduction to working with sheet metal, using a manual cutting technique. Sheet metal is available in many gauges: the medium-weight sheet used here is sturdy enough to hold its shape but thin enough to cut with scissors or, preferably, specific sheet-metal shears. Thin sheet metal and wire usually come rolled and you can buy them at jewelry-making supply stores, art and craft stores, and online.

Metalwork is a craft that generally requires the use of specialized tools and equipment, but this wall hanging has been designed to keep those to a minimum. You can go up or down in gauge but be warned, any thinner and you risk denting the metal quite easily and anything thicker will require more particular tools. Besides pipe cutters (and pipe), which are available at hardware stores, all other tools can be purchased from the same outlets as sheet metal and wire.

The best advice when working with metal is to wear gloves, particularly when you will be dodging the sharp edges of sheet metal. They will also help you avoid leaving fingerprints on the shiny surface, minimizing the need for polishing the finished piece. Choose gloves that are thick enough to protect your hands while still allowing your fingertips to feel and work with the material easily.

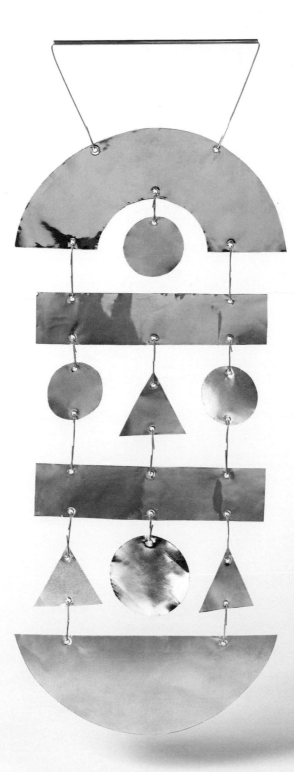

MATERIALS

› Printed template online:
  www.tamaramaynes.com
› 30-gauge copper sheet metal
› 24-gauge copper wire
› 6-gauge copper pipe
› Spray-on clear lacquer for metal

TOOLS

› Fitted cotton gloves
› Pencil
› Sheet metal shears
› Ruler
› Metal hole punch
› Pipe cutters
› Wire cutters
› Chain-nose pliers with non-serrated jaws
› Polishing cloth

PREPARE

1 / Download the template and print out onto plain 11 x 17 in (A3) paper at 100%.

2 / Wear protective gloves to unroll and carefully flatten out sheet metal. Lay it on an unmarked flat surface under a stack of heavy books overnight.

3 / To prepare copper wire for joining metal pieces, cut fourteen 3 in (7.5 cm) lengths of wire.

4 / To prepare copper wire for hanging, cut one 13 in (32 cm) length of wire.

5 / To prepare copper pipe, cut one 5 in (13 cm) length using pipe cutters.

MAKE

1 / Cut out the paper template pieces, place on the metal sheet, and trace around them with a pencil, also marking the spots where holes are to be punched. Wearing protective gloves, use sheet metal shears to carefully cut out the individual metal pieces.

2 / To make holes, use a metal hole punch to gently pierce metal pieces where indicated on the template.

3 / To join the metal pieces, thread the short wire lengths through the punched holes, as indicated in the photograph. Use pliers to fold one wire end over and back onto itself to secure. Thread the other end of the wire through the corresponding hole. Keep all the folded wire ends to the back.

4 / To hang, first thread the 13 in (32 cm) wire length through the pipe. Thread the ends through the holes at top left and right of the top curved metal piece, as shown on page 83. Use pliers to fold the wire ends over to secure, as before.

5 / To polish, gently clean entire hanging with polishing cloth.

6 / Immediately after cleaning, hang outside and spray with lacquer to seal as per manufacturer's instructions. This step will help prevent the copper from oxidizing.

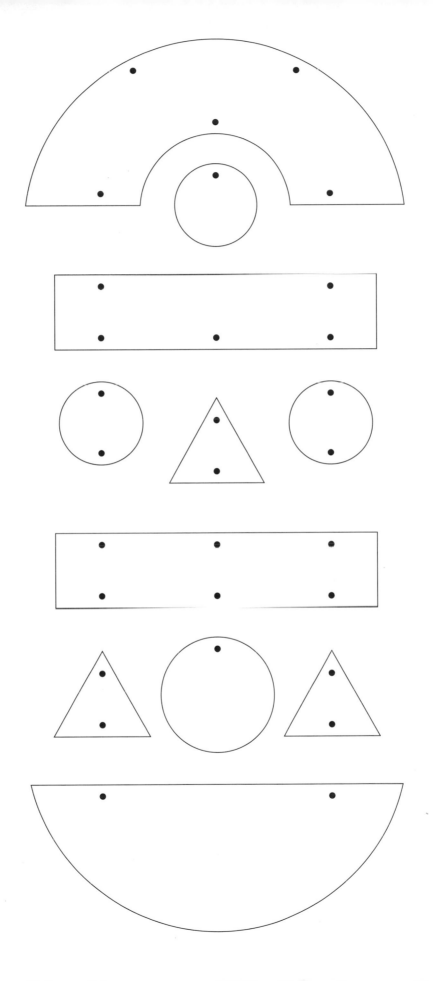

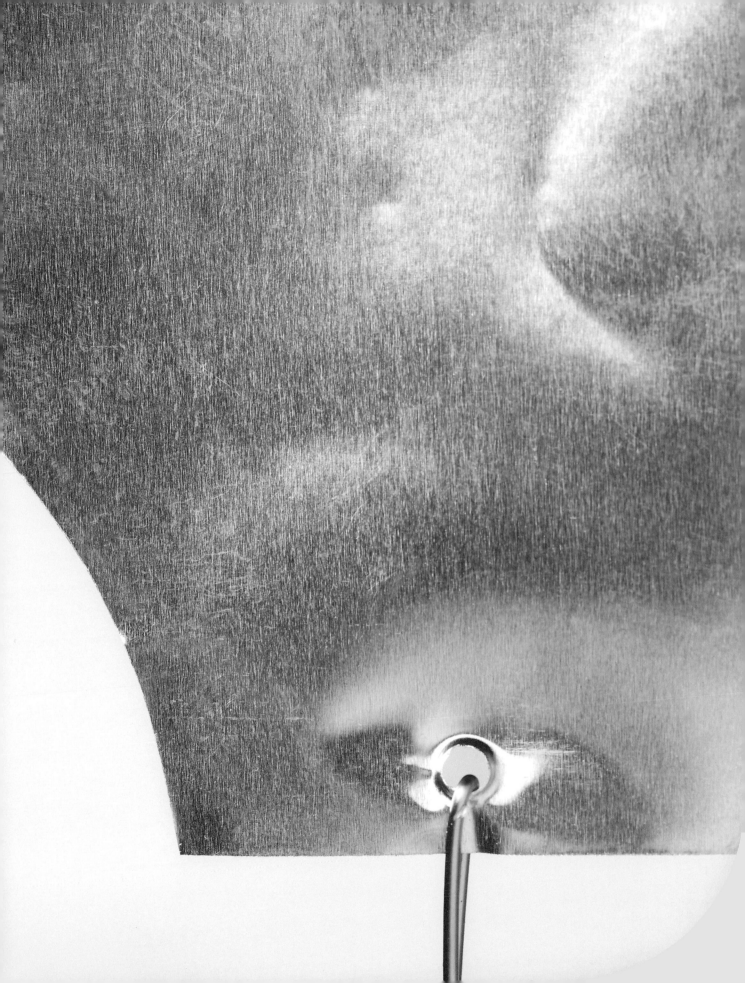

OBJECTS
chapter five

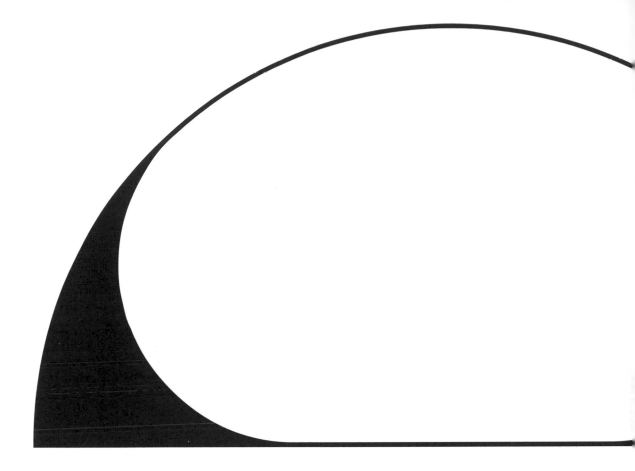

Dust collectors? I think not! Beautifully crafted objects that often have no function deserve far greater credit than many give them. Spanning more crafts than any other aspect of a space, objects offer the maker THE most wondrous opportunity for an adventure (not to mention a home with authentic souvenirs).

As a maker, I naturally veer toward decorative, non-functional pieces. I always have; I think it stems from growing up on a sheep and cattle farm that spent much of its time in drought. Although it was stunningly beautiful, I could never shake the feeling that the dry, dusty hills and paddocks, coupled with the utilitarian aspects of a working farm, felt harsh, aesthetically. To counterbalance this I subconsciously found myself inclined towards the decorative aspect of a space over its functional one. While I now understand this motivation as ingrained, I also appreciate that it developed my respect for craftsmanship, good design, and quality materials.

The objects in most homes are made up of mementos collected from travels, work, relationships, and life, and, of course, while they all have meaning, those that have been made by the occupant hold an added layer of experience. Conveying personal inspirations and skill, they have the power to take the maker with them to a place not found on any map. The message behind object making is explained here by the output of a collection of makers who explore paper art, weaving, metalwork, fabric mâché, woodwork, leatherwork, and glass blowing. Their sense of adventure in making is glaringly obvious, appointing them as those whose work resonates with me the most.

**Scandinavian
Design**

"WORKING WITH PAPER IS MY PASSION. I FIND IT AN ENDLESSLY INVENTIVE MEDIUM. WHEN I MAKE I GO WITH THE FLOW AND DON'T GET CAUGHT UP IN RIGHT OR WRONG. I DON'T LIKE TO REPEAT MYSELF SO I TRY TO APPROACH EACH NEW PIECE IN A UNIQUE WAY."

BENJA HARNEY, PAPER ENGINEER (SYDNEY, AUSTRALIA)

Life-size ice skates sculpted from lightweight paper card

"Weaving with plant materials connects me to the seasons and the natural world. Random weaving is a contemporary technique adapted from Japanese interlacing. It lets go of the drive for symmetry and embraces organic form, sweeping rhythm and texture."

**HARRIET GOODALL, FIBER ARTIST & BASKET MAKER
(ROBERTSON, AUSTRALIA)**

Random weave basket, using indigo-dyed core cane

"I STARTED WELDING AND WORKING WITH PRECIOUS
METALS AS A SCULPTOR, CREATING WORKS THAT
ARE DIFFICULT TO SEE HOW THEY HAVE BEEN
PRODUCED. IT'S VERY HARD WORK
BUT THE RESULTS ARE WORTH IT."

**BEN BLAKEBROUGH, DESIGNER & MAKER
(SOUTHERN HIGHLANDS, AUSTRALIA)**

Welded brass candelabra finished with a blackened patina

"Working with glass is the single most amazing thing I have ever done. I make with my heart and hands and feel confident that, even if my head is not sure what we are making, my hands will lead the way."

AMANDA DZIEDZIC, GLASS BLOWER (MELBOURNE, AUSTRALIA)

Hand-blown colored glass vessels

Q&A

Maker to Maker with...

Georgina Brown,
textile & papier-mâché artist

(Sydney, Australia)

TM: Georgina, describe your sculptural fabric mâché.
GB: These pieces are a selection of bowls and shapes patched with vintage fabrics, Japanese boro, and vintage tickings.

TM: Can you explain the technique?
GB: I start with a shaped piece of cardboard, layer and layer papier-mâché and then, when the shape and weight is working, I add a final layer of fabric patched over the top.

TM: Sounds messy . . . Where do you make?
GB: We live in a shoebox! I grab space wherever I can. I'm lucky to have a long sunny window ledge to dry pieces on.

TM: Does indigo blue always play a starring role in your pieces?
GB: I am always drawn back to blue and, as my work has a strong Japanese influence,

indigo and boro are a perfect match. I love to add inky blacks and chocolate ikat in here and there . . . but, yes, it is all about the blue.

TM: Have you always been a maker?
GB: I started in a very different field, as a makeup artist for TV and film. After u stint living in New York I turned to design and there was no turning back.

TM: How has it changed things for you?
GB: Making is essential in my life. It gives me the balance to do all the other stuff.

TM: Can you describe what happens when you make?
GB: I get lost in the process.

TM: What do you think papier/fabric mâché brings to a space?
GB: An organic sculptural quality.

Constructed wood gems using mitered and beveled plywood / Nick Pearce

"

I find it humbling to work closely with a material that was part of nature, that has often stood for many more years than I have. The process of refining something wild into something that will be loved for many more years to come is rewarding.

"

NICK PEARCE, FURNITURE & OBJECT MAKER
(MELBOURNE, AUSTRALIA)

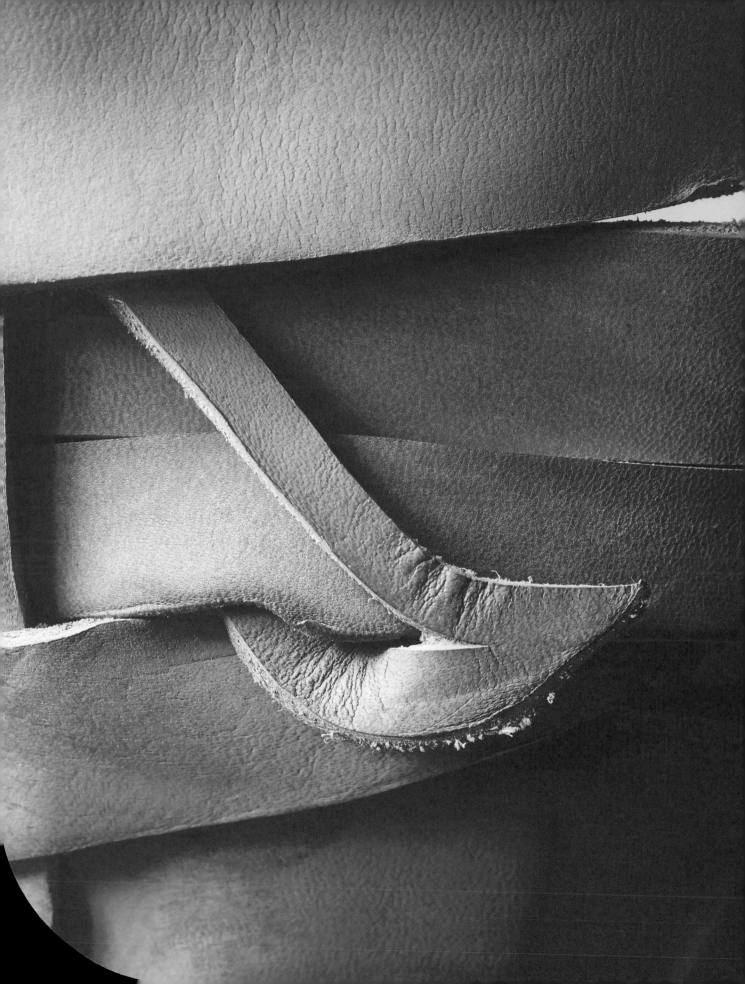

"I THINK THE NEED TO CREATE IS HARDWIRED INTO OUR DNA AS HUMAN BEINGS. WORKING WITH LEATHER FASCINATES ME DAILY. I AM ALWAYS DISCOVERING NEW WAYS TO MANIPULATE IT SO THAT I CAN CREATE UNEXPECTED OBJECTS."

JENNIFER STILWELL, LEATHER ARTISAN
(NEW YORK, USA)

*Cuir bouilli (boiled) molded planter
made from naked vegetable-tan leather*

"MY TURNED WOODEN DOLLS ARE INFLUENCED BY THOSE OF THE AVANT-GARDE ARTISTS OF THE TWENTIETH CENTURY AND ARE CREATED AS PART OF THAT TRADITION. IT IS IMPORTANT TO ME THAT THE WORK I MAKE SITS WELL BESIDE THOSE I'M INSPIRED BY."

SARAH K, DESIGNER, MAKER, & CURATOR (SOUTHERN HIGHLANDS, AUSTRALIA)

Hand-painted dolls made from turned wood offcuts

"WORKING WITH SUSTAINABLE WOOD
IS REALLY GRATIFYING. IT'S BEAUTIFUL,
NATURAL, RENEWABLE, READILY
AVAILABLE, AND OFFERS A VARIETY
OF COLORS AND PATTERNS."

**COCO REYNOLDS, LIGHTING & FURNITURE DESIGNER
(SYDNEY, AUSTRALIA)**

"PLASTIC IS A SUPER-MATERIAL AND SHOULD BE
CONSIDERED A VALUABLE COMMODITY. IT HAS
THIS ABILITY TO LAST FOREVER SO, INSTEAD OF
CREATING PIECES INTENDED FOR A SINGLE USE
ONLY TO BE SUBSEQUENTLY DISCARDED, WE
MAKE THINGS THAT NEED TO BE CARED
FOR AND KEPT."

**SARAH K & LIANE ROSSLER, FOUNDERS OF SUPERCYCLERS INTERNATIONAL
SUSTAINABLE DESIGN COLLECTIVE (SYDNEY, AUSTRALIA)**

"I LIKE TO BE ABLE TO TRACE EVERY ELEMENT
OF THE PIECE BACK TO ITS SOURCE, PREFERABLY
HARVESTING, FORAGING, AND COLLECTING THE
MATERIALS MYSELF."

**HARRIET GOODALL, FIBER ARTIST & BASKET MAKER
(ROBERTSON, AUSTRALIA)**

a word on...
SUSTAINABLE MAKING

Making can mean chewing through raw materials, relying on resources such as energy, and ultimately adding to landfill. This leaves the maker with a responsibility to question their practice and how they might make choices that support sustainability and challenge perceptions of what is valuable. Being aware of and accountable for sustainability isn't as hard as you might think and thankfully there are incredible opportunities to incorporate it.

Supporting sustainability can mean choosing to use raw materials that have been certified sustainable, discarded as waste, or sourced locally—effectively reducing the emissions involved with freight. Many makers are now offsetting the fossil fuel emissions used in the manufacture of their product by donating to environmental causes focused on developing renewable energy and sustainability. Others adopt advances in production that allow them to reuse waste water, for example. The other aspect of sustainable making, which can drastically reduce waste, is finding ways to place greater worth on the maker's output. Being transparent about your making process is a great place to start to encourage the concept of value. Including sustainability in a practice might be a daunting thought, but it is becoming increasingly essential, and achievable, and will most definitely result in adding further uniqueness to the maker's output.

PROJECT Nº2
wirework 3D silhouettes

The template on the following pages is a guide only and not to scale. A complete ready-to-print template can be found at www.tamaramaynes.com.

Wirework is a fond inclusion in my personal practice. I love that the finished work looks so simple, yet requires more technique and skill than most people realize (until they begin exploring it). The main response I get when teaching wirework is "I had no idea how challenging it would be!" Having said that, patience and commitment to learning this craft, coupled with experience working the material, will have you making quality wirework. To get you started, this project focuses on making bends and curves using a "dead soft" enameled copper wire—dead soft being the term used to refer to the hardness of the wire. I have specified 12- or 14-gauge—if you are an absolute beginner, the 14-gauge will be easier to work. Be aware that as the gauge size gets higher, the wire gets thinner, so a 12-gauge is .08 in (2.1 mm) thick while a 14-gauge is .06 in (1.6 mm) thick. This wire can be bought easily at jewelery-making supply stores, craft and art stores, and online.

The pliers required for this project are basic and consist of: chain-nose with non-serrated jaws (their smooth jaws protect the wire from being scratched when grasped); nylon-jaw flat-nose pliers (whose jaws have a larger surface area and are even more gentle on the wire's surface); and flush-cutting wire cutters, which make a good clean cut that leaves no sharp edges. All can be bought wherever you purchase the wire. Take this project slowly and, if possible, buy some extra wire to play around with first, perhaps an even thinner 16-gauge sample. Working with pliers successfully also takes practice, but stick with it.

MATERIALS

› Printed template online: www.tamaramaynes.com
› 12- or 14-gauge round, dead soft, enameled copper craft wire (for contrast, use 1 short spool each of tarnish resistant brass and natural copper)

TOOLS

› Non-permanent marker with fine-pointed tip (ensure it will not mark wire permanently)
› Chain-nose pliers with non-serrated jaw
› Flush-cutting wire cutters
› Nylon-jaw flat-nose pliers
› Polishing cloth, for final cleaning if necessary

PREPARE

1 / Download the template and print out onto plain 11 x 17 in (A3) paper at 100%.

2 / Gently unfurl the first 12 in (30 cm) wire. Do not cut the wire, but leave it on the spool and continue to unfurl it in sections as you work.

MAKE

1 / Lay template on the work surface. Lay the section of unfurled wire on top of the template and, starting at either end of the template, use it as a guide while you bend the wire to mirror the pattern. Keep the wire flat and untwisted while you form the outline, laying it over the template regularly to make sure it matches.

2 / To make angles, transfer the bend spot indicators (in gray on the pattern) to the wire with the marker. Grip the jaws of the chain-nose pliers around the wire just beside the mark and bend the wire with your fingers to form the angle.

3 / To make curves, manipulate the wire between your thumb and index finger.

4 / To straighten the wire, if necessary, place the wire between the jaws of the flat-nose pliers and run them along the wire gently until it is straight.

5 / To finish the silhouette, transfer the end point from the pattern onto the wire with the marker. Use wire cutters to cut the wire and remove spool.

6 / To form the 3D aspect, transfer all the brown bend spot indicators from the pattern to the wire with the marker. Grip the jaws of the chain-nose pliers around the wire just beside the first mark and bend. This bend should be perpendicular so that the wire form is no longer flat. Repeat for each brown mark, forming the "top" and "bottom" of the silhouette.

7 / To secure wire at beginning and end, transfer the black bend spot indicators from the pattern to the wire with the marker. Grip the jaws of the chain-nose pliers around the wire just beside the mark and bend the small section back on itself so it is almost parallel and forms a hook. Place the complete wire section that meets or crosses this point inside the hook. Finally, place the jaws of the flat-nose pliers around the hook and lock it by gently squeezing it closed.

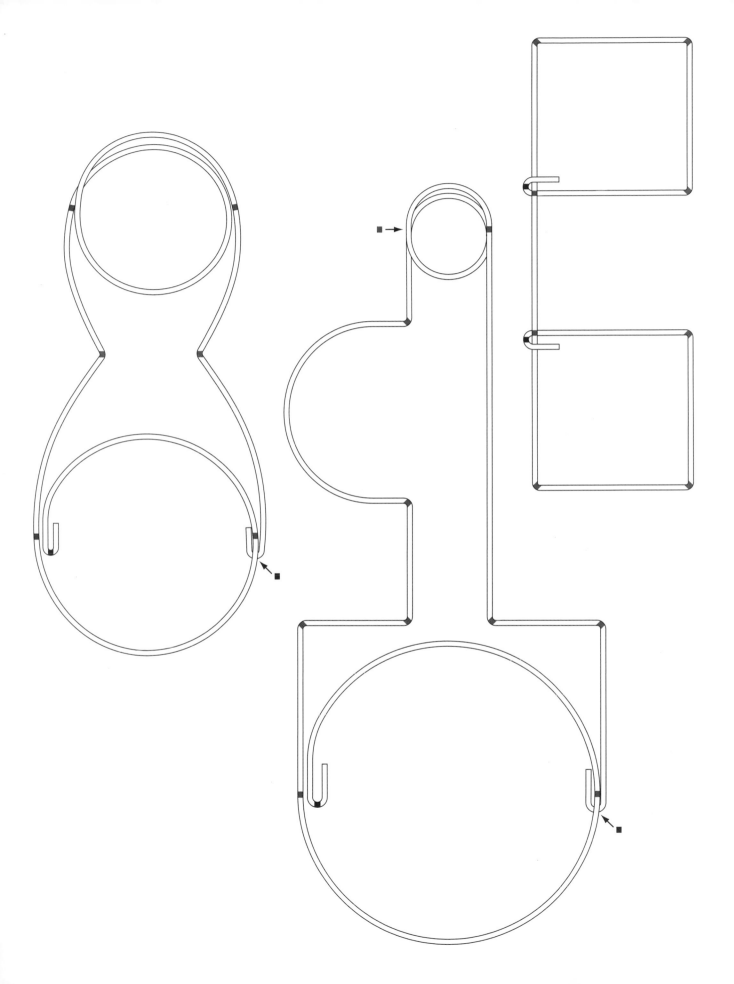

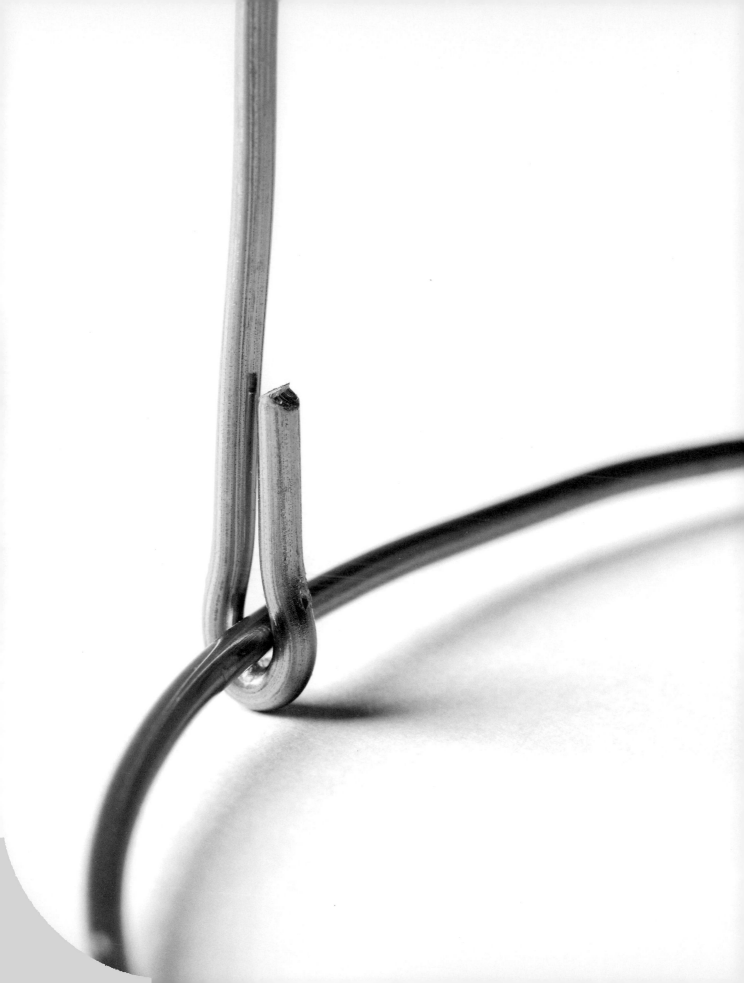

TEXTILES
chapter six

From providing warmth, comfort, and protection, to pleasing the eye with color, pattern, and texture, textiles play an incredibly diverse role in our spaces. Just as the possibilities for self-expression offered to the maker are endless, so too is the potential to weave some real magic into your home.

Have you ever slept under a patchwork quilt? I have, and it rendered me the loveliest sense of calm. It was as if I were bundled not only in the softest cotton, but also in tradition and meaning. Quilting is an extremely old textile practice, and the techniques and designs have been cherished throughout times of wealth, pilgrimages, wars, and great depressions. Often crafted out of necessity and thrift, the making of a quilt also served to mark great occasions and represent generations of family. So all these aspects envelop you when your bed is made warm with a patchwork quilt. Somehow, quite magically, all this is woven into the fibers, sewn in with every stitch.

Although most textile practices have been around for centuries, they have the enchanting ability, no matter how modern the approach to technique or materials, or how unique the maker, to not only carry history and tradition but to allow it to shine through. Whether it's present in the yarn, fabric, process, or design, it's there and can bring a source of real depth and energy into any space.

Making textiles is rewarding on so many levels and as a maker I believe the more aware you are of the story behind your chosen practice the stronger a connection you can form. What comes from this connection is up to your individuality, craftsmanship, and willingness to experiment. The makers' work featured in this chapter spans rug making, textile surface decoration such as shibori and appliqué, quilting, knitting, and good old sewing. Passionate about their crafts, these makers express the ability of modern textiles to add a level of ceremony and nostalgia to any space.

I started knitting after I had a dream
in which a loud booming voice told me
that I was 'to knit blankets and they
need to be big.' I had been searching for
something creative for some time and so
when the answer finally came
I didn't dare question it.

**JACQUELINE FINK, LARGE-SCALE KNITTER
(SYDNEY, AUSTRALIA)**

Large-scale knitted throw, using garter stitch on felted merino wool yarn /
Jacqueline Fink

"My connection to textiles is my love for tactility. I am happiest making my own world of textiles —creating something just from yarns."

MAE ENGELGEER, TEXTILE DESIGNER (AMSTERDAM, NETHERLANDS)

Berber- and Boucherouite-inspired carpet rug, hand-knotted from pure wool

"WHEN I MAKE MY SWANS I THINK OF THEM AS CHARACTERS. I PUT A LOT OF EFFORT INTO THE LITTLE FINISHING TOUCHES, INCLUDING DREAMING UP WHAT THEIR NAMES WILL BE!"

KARA HYNES, MAKER (BRISBANE, AUSTRALIA)

Violet the swan—sewn, quilted, and embroidered using wool, felt, cotton, and linen

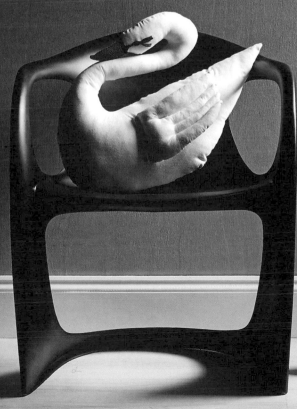

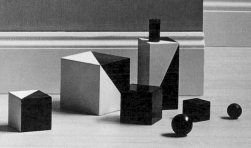

"

Designing and dyeing the velvet colors for our textiles is one of the most joyful parts of the process: finding the exact nuance and then the next color to combine with it.

"

ADAM GISTEDT & VIKTORIA NYGREN, TEXTILE DESIGNERS
(STOCKHOLM, SWEDEN)

*Linen cushion with appliquéd
and embroidered silk velvet /
Adam Gistedt & Viktoria Nygren*

*Full-grain leather hide, hand-bound and dyed using the Japanese shibori technique /
Pepa Martin & Karen Davis*

"Working with shibori means there is never any shortage of ideas or directions to go in. We started working with leather because we wanted to explore this ancient technique on different textures and in new ways."

PEPA MARTIN & KAREN DAVIS, TEXTILE DESIGNERS
(SYDNEY, AUSTRALIA)

Q&A

Maker to Maker with...

Meg Callahan, patchwork quilter

(Rhode Island, USA)

TM: Meg, describe your modern quilt.
MC: The bold graphics, influenced by both the natural and man-made, are digitally printed on organic cotton. Industrial machine stitching creates the quilt's textured pattern.

TM: You generally practice traditional patchwork quilting, but you teamed up with contemporary New York design showroom and manufacturer Matter to merge tradition with technology for this piece?
MC: Inspired by traditional American quilting and my Oklahoma roots, the quilts I created with Matter use modern technology to express age-old sentiments of comfort and home.

TM: What is your process when making a quilt using traditional techniques?
MC: Patchworked pieces are made one at a time, and have an extensive amount of handwork in them. Composed of small, cut pieces of fabric that are sewn together to construct a pattern, depending on its complexity, one quilt can take six to ten weeks to complete. However, it's a process that takes more attention than time, and the more "present" I am in making, the more efficient the process.

TM: When and why did you start quilting?
MC: I started in school and haven't stopped since. Making with my hands is an extremely fulfilling and humbling experience. Mostly humbling, because it makes me aware of all the skill and patience other makers have.

TM: What happens when you make?
MC: I am equal parts happy / frustrated / inspired / motivated / elated / exhausted.

TM: Where do you make?
MC: My studio: a BIG table, a sewing machine, and tons of scissors.

TM: What do you think patchwork quilts bring to a space?
MC: All textiles bring warmth to a space.

"WE WORK WITH EACH OTHER'S STRENGTHS AND SUPPORT ONE ANOTHER, TRUSTING OUR INDIVIDUAL CREATIVE ENERGIES THROUGH BEAUTIFUL COLORS, NATURAL FIBERS, AND HAND PROCESSES. AS A RESULT, OUR TEXTILES BRING VIBRANCY AND UNIQUENESS TO A SPACE."

JOANNA FOWLES & KATE BANAZI, COLLABORATING TEXTILE DESIGNERS (SYDNEY, AUSTRALIA)

Linen curtain drop, hand-painted in indigo

"I SPEND MOST OF MY TIME RESEARCHING, EXPERIMENTING, AND PRODUCING THE DYES AND FABRICS FOR MY WORK. WHEN THE TIME COMES TO MAKE A QUILT, I'M CONFIDENT OF KEEPING THINGS SIMPLE BECAUSE THE RAW MATERIALS STAND ON THEIR OWN. IF YOU'RE FEELING STUCK CREATIVELY, WORK TO IMPROVE YOUR MATERIALS. THERE'S A SPRING OF INSPIRATION THERE."

MAURA AMBROSE, TEXTILE ARTIST & QUILTER
(TEXAS, USA)

"WHEN I MAKE, I PUT MY EGO TO THE SIDE AND ALLOW THE MATERIALS TO SPEAK WITH A STRONG VOICE."

MARYANNE MOODIE, TAPESTRY WEAVER
(NEW YORK, USA)

"IT'S IMPORTANT TO WORK WITH MATERIALS YOU LOVE AND FEEL A CONNECTION WITH. YOUR PASSION FOR WHAT YOU DO WILL COME THROUGH IN YOUR WORK."

VICTORIA PEMBERTON, TEXTILE ARTIST
(MELBOURNE, AUSTRALIA)

a word on...
RAW MATERIALS

All makers love raw materials, but makers of textiles seem to go the extra mile. As a self-confessed textile lover, I have been known to store tens of boxes of fabrics for years. I couldn't bear to part with them or the idea of what I would eventually make with them. Many years ago, when I was focusing on making bespoke textiles, my home studio consisted of floor-to-ceiling shelving housing color-blocked vintage fabrics, much like the one my mother kept when I was growing up. Whatever the maker's practice, a love of, addiction to, and passion for raw materials is just part of life. Many makers – particularly those working with textiles – go one step further and create their own raw materials, such as knitters who spin their own wool, or quilters who dye fabrics to achieve the exact color they envision. Apart from the control gained from creating raw materials, and the joy of collecting, just having a selection on hand enables a more unplanned approach to making that can work wonders to promote inspiration and individuality.

PROJECT Nº 3
woven table runner

If you are interested in weaving, this table runner project will give you a taste of what you can achieve with very limited tools, basic materials, and some patience. Using the principles behind tapestry weaving or weft-facing weaving (decorative weaving as opposed to the production of fabric) this piece repeats a simple under-over process where the warp (the longitudinal yarn attached to the loom) is hidden under the weft (the yarn being worked). The ropes used for warp and weft are both standard affordable hardware ropes, while the metallic yarn used to lock the warp at both ends is intended for fiber crafts and can be found at craft stores and online.

As with many crafts, basic weaving tools can often be replaced by existing household items. I actually wove this piece on a makeshift loom that was the frame of a small desk whose table top had been removed. It worked perfectly well, but for the purpose of this weaving introduction I encourage you to seek out a basic frame loom, to which you will attach the warp. Similarly, a shed stick, which is used to create a space, or "shed," between the warp in order to thread the weft through, can be replaced with a ruler. Usually you would also need a thin wooden tool called a shuttle to contain the long lengths of weft as you feed them through the warp, but because this project uses thick rope, using a shuttle becomes more problematic than helpful. (I just used my fingers.) These weaving tools are all available from craft supply stores.

Weaving is a lengthy process and, because there's nothing more deflating than an unfinished project, I feel compelled to push you to consider the dimensions of your finished runner before you purchase tools and materials. A frame loom won't allow you to weave a finished piece any larger than its dimensions, so for this reason alone, planning is essential.

MATERIALS

› 89 ft (27 m) of ¼ in (5 mm) thick unbleached cotton rope
› 115 ft (35 m) of ¼ in (5 mm) thick white synthetic rope
› Ball of metallic silver yarn

TOOLS

› Scissors
› Tape measure
› 16 x 28 in (40 x 70 cm) basic frame loom
› Shed stick or ruler
› Long-nose pliers
› Lighter or matches

PREPARE

1 / To prepare warp, cut cotton rope into twenty-four 43 in (1.1 m) lengths.

2 / To prepare weft, cut synthetic rope into ten 138 in (3.5 m) lengths. Seal the cut ends with a flame close enough to melt them, to prevent fraying.

3 / To prepare or "warp" the loom, beginning in the middle of the loom, tie one piece of cotton rope securely to the top and bottom rungs on its long side. Repeat for the remaining lengths of cotton rope, leaving approximately ¼ in (5 mm) between each. Ensure each is pulled taut with a similar tension.

4 / To prepare metallic thread, cut eleven 24 in (60 cm) lengths.

5 / To prepare for weaving, sit the bottom rung of the loom on your lap and rest the top rung against a table.

MAKE

1 / To begin weaving, take the shed stick and thread it horizontally across and through the warp two at a time—over two, under two, over two, etc. Next, flip the stick on its side, creating a shed between the warps. While the shed is open, take the first length of weft and thread it through the space from left to right, leaving a 6 in (15 cm) loose end at the start. Then, flip the stick flat again and use it to push the first row of woven weft down so it sits close to and in line with the bottom rung of the loom that is resting on your lap.

2 / To resume weaving, working away from yourself, insert the stick through the warp as before but this time start with under instead of over. Next, flip the stick as before to create a shed. Thread the existing weft thread through the shed, this time going from right to left. Finally, flip the stick again and, before removing it from the warp, use it to gently push the second row of woven weft down so it sits snugly along the top of the first.

3 / To continue weaving, repeat step 2, alternating between threading the weft from the left and right, until your weft thread has no less than 6 in (15 cm) remaining and the end is trailing out the back of your work. As you weave you will notice your weft has a tendency to draw the width of your piece inwards which, if left unchecked, will see the width of your finished piece (approximately

9 in/22 cm) vary along its length. To ensure this doesn't happen, tie a short unwanted rope offcut to the outside left rung of the loom across to the first warp and repeat on the right. Slide these ropes up and down when necessary, using it as a guide to correct width as you weave.

4 / To start a new weft thread, insert it where the last one ends, leaving a 6 in (15 cm) loose end trailing out the back of your work, and continue weaving.

5 / To complete weaving, repeat steps 2 to 4 until the warp is covered and the woven weft sits close to the top rung of the loom, measuring approximately 23 in (58 cm) long. Untie the warps to free the finished weaving from the loom.

6 / To secure the 6 in (15 cm) weft ends trailing at the back, and also at the start and finish, turn the weaving over and use the pliers to thread each tail through and along the underside of the weaving.

7 / To make fringed ends, measure and cut the loose warp hanging from each end of the weaving to 8 in (20 cm) long.

8 / To secure fringe, first take one length of metallic yarn and join the warps by wrapping the thread around the base of the second and third warps on one side. Knot securely. Repeat this process for every two warps along both ends of the weaving, leaving the outer warp on either side of each end unsecured. Without securing the fringe, the "unlocked" weft will begin to loosen and unravel over time.

CERAMICS
chapter seven

Ceramics in a space are most often associated with sharing meals or honoring flora. Both acts can be incredibly beautiful, personal, and memorable, as can the ceramics that facilitate them. I clearly remember being given a modern ceramic vase that had been hand-built and sold by a Sydney ceramicist at a local design market for my sixteenth birthday. It was the first vase I ever owned and I recall its shape and glazed pattern distinctively; it took a place of pride in my bedroom and paved the way for an addiction to ceramics that is alive and well today. Not a week goes by when I don't buy fresh cut flowers and spend far too long choosing a vase from my collection in which to display them. The ceramic piece itself, the act of filling it with flowers and the energy that emanates from that area in my home bring me the simplest joy.

The act of making ceramics is just as significant as the enjoyment of the finished piece and I have fond childhood memories of learning to throw clay on the potter's wheel on Saturday mornings. Making ceramics is an ever-evolving experiment and, in the words of many ceramicists, a roller coaster of emotions. More than any other making medium, ceramics allows your personality and that of the piece to shine through, warts and all. The ceramicists whose work I've focused on in this chapter cover techniques such as hand-built, wheel-thrown, and slip-cast pottery, using stoneware and porcelain clay bodies, and illustrate a process that's incredibly individual and organic with a set of rules that any maker should break—once they've spent some time learning them!

"MY PLATES AND CUPS ARE HAND-BUILT WITH PORCELAIN, AND THEN ETCHED WITH PATTERNS—PATTERNS THAT USUALLY REPEAT, OR REAPPEAR ELSEWHERE, DEPENDING ON WHERE THEY TAKE ME."

SUZANNE SULLIVAN, CERAMICIST (NEW YORK, USA)

Hand-built, etched, and glazed porcelain tableware

"I often feel as if I'm illustrating in clay: I make shapes and then stamp or draw into it using carved wooden pegs. If it's not working, I can smooth it over again."

**STELLA BAGGOTT, CERAMIC DESIGNER & MAKER
(LONDON, UK)**

Hand-built Staffordshire stoneware vase with matte white glaze

Q&A

Maker to Maker with...

Alison Fraser, ceramicist

(Southern Highlands, Australia)

TM: Alison, describe your textured ceramics.
AF: These bottle forms are hand-built with a heavily grogged stoneware clay and finished with shino glaze.

TM: What is your process and how do you achieve such a distinctive glaze?
AF: I roll the clay into slabs and then cut and shape them to create the form. I don't use a potter's wheel at all. I mix the matte shino glaze myself; it responds beautifully to the iron in the clay, hence the rust.

TM: Why did you become a ceramicist?
AF: After a career in graphic design I longed to do something more self-directed and tactile. I enjoy the process and feel of the clay.

TM: What happens when you make?
AF: I go into "the zone," with thoughts of the outside world dropping away. There is little planning and the forms usually spring forth spontaneously. I do have a warehouse in my head of structures, colors, and textures that I would like to explore and they take turns to leap out and have control of my hands.

TM: Does your "warehouse" include a bond with the makers of the past?
AF: I enjoy the link to my creative forebears and hope that this ancient connection extends into the contemporary homes my pieces go into.

TM: What do you think ceramics bring to a modern space?
AF: Warmth, humanity, and, most importantly, stories.

TM: Where do you make?
AF: I started out on the dining room table, lounge room floor, and in the garden. Then I had a studio that was packed up every time we had a house guest, then a tiny cobwebby old garage, but now I am about to "graduate" to a 42-square-meter purpose-built studio space that will be all mine, mine, mine...

"
These bottles use a 'crawling' glaze that clumps during firing. Many potters would reject such severe crawling, but I like it
"

ALISON FRASER, CERAMICIST
(SOUTHERN HIGHLANDS, AUSTRALIA)

Hand-built stoneware bottles using shino glaze

Wheel-thrown, hand-built stoneware tableware with hand-dipped glazes / Bridget Bodenham

"MAKING GIVES ME A PURPOSE IN LIFE. IT IS THE MOST HUMBLING GIFT TO CREATE A CUP AND THEN OFFER IT TO A LOVED ONE TO DRINK FROM."

BRIDGET BODENHAM, POTTER (HEPBURN SPRINGS, AUSTRALIA)

"

Working with clay is one of the most peaceful, grounding things I have known. There's just something about it. It grows on you very quickly...

"

LARA HUTTON, STYLIST, ARTIST & CERAMICIST
(SYDNEY, AUSTRALIA)

Hand-built porcelain tableware & vessels

"Handmade pottery brings a unique personality to a space. Sgraffito and wax-resist techniques combine with my favorite bright blue, cobalt oxide, to create one-of-a-kind pieces that have my fingerprint on them, literally."

LAUREN BAMFORD,
PHOTOGRAPHER & MOONLIGHTING CERAMICIST
(MELBOURNE, AUSTRALIA)

Hand-built & slip-cast stoneware & porcelain tableware

"MY STUDIO IS IN A SMALL FOREST,
COMPLETELY SURROUNDED BY THE VERY
NATURE THAT INSPIRES MY CERAMICS. THE
EXTERIOR IS PAINTED A SMOKY SHADE OF
BLUE/BLACK THAT BLENDS IN WITH THE
SURROUNDING LANDSCAPE. THE INTERIOR
IS BRIGHT WHITE COMBINED WITH NATURAL
WOOD AND VARYING SHADES OF BLUE
FURNISHINGS, ALL HANDMADE. IT'S A TRULY
INSPIRATIONAL SPACE TO WORK IN."

MICHELE MICHAEL, CERAMICIST
(MAINE, USA)

"I LIKE TO KEEP MY STUDIO FUN AND
INSPIRING, SO IT FEELS MORE LIKE A
PLAY SPACE THAN A WORK SPACE."

SALLY ENGLAND, FIBER ARTIST
(MICHIGAN, USA)

"I WORK IN A SUNNY LIGHT-FILLED
ROOM STACKED FULL OF MOLDS AND
SCULPTURES. HIGH SHELVES HOLD
ROWS OF MY PLASTER BUSTS, WHO
KEEP THEIR EAGLE EYES ON ME
WHILE I MAKE."

KATHY DALWOOD, PLASTER SCULPTOR
(LONDON, UK)

a word on...
SPACE FOR MAKING

Making in general can be a messy affair, but making ceramics is downright dirty work. Remember making mud pies as a kid? Well, take that memory, clean it up with some adult awareness and bring it indoors. Suffice to say that, like any maker, a ceramicist can make anywhere but will eventually require and be forever grateful for a delegated workspace of some description—one that is easily cleaned or ok to remain covered in clay. This doesn't mean every ceramicist needs an idyllic outdoor studio flooded with natural light, decked out with floor-to-ceiling shelving and a kiln. This would be incredible, of course, and certainly something to aspire to, but the reality for most of us just starting out is a corner of the kitchen in the still of the late evening, or a crumbling garden shed that's shared with undesirable wildlife. Oddly enough, this is often part of the joy of making.

PROJECT Nº 4
no-fire clay vessel

This ceramic project uses no-fire, air-dry clay, partly because it's a great alternative to kiln firing (and, let's face it, not every aspiring ceramicist has access to a kiln). Air-dry clay has excellent plasticity, making it very easy to work with. The downside is that your finished piece won't be waterproof or food safe, so you will only be able to produce decorative pieces. A word of warning regarding color: fresh from its packaging, white air-dry clay will almost always appear a shade of gray putty, but it does transform to a beautiful warm white the longer it is left to dry. It is available from pottery supply stores, art stores, and online and, as with any raw material, it's wise to spend as much as you can afford to achieve the best result. Having said that, even the best air-dry clays are usually very reasonably priced.

You probably already own the tools for this project, so no real sourcing or outlay is necessary. What you will have to get your hands on is a faceted cut-glass bowl (or something similar) with a raised pattern on its surface that can be imprinted into the clay. Second-hand shops usually carry them by the truckload.

When working with clay, be prepared for your work area, and yourself, to get dirty. Keep water on hand because you may well lose yourself in the process and your clay might start to dry out before you've finished forming it.

MATERIALS

› 1 lb 2 oz (500 g)
  white air-dry clay
› Acrylic paints in white,
  cream, nude, gray, caramel,
  gold, & silver
› Spray-on clear matte sealant

TOOLS

› Knife
› Rolling pin
› Clean, untextured working
  surface (check the clay manufacturer's
  recommendations to prevent sticking)
› Faceted cut-glass bowl, dust-free
› Cooling tray
› Artist paintbrush

PREPARE

1 / To prepare the clay, slice a handful from the block and re-seal it so the remaining clay doesn't dry out. Knead the clay on the working surface until it's soft and workable (like dough) to remove any air bubbles. Work into a smooth ball, wetting your hands just slightly to keep the clay moist if necessary. Use the rolling pin to work the ball out into a ¼ in (5 mm) thick, flat, smooth circle.

2 / Place the cut-glass bowl upside down on your working surface.

MAKE

1 / To imprint the clay, peel the rolled-out clay carefully off the working surface and lay it over the upturned bowl. Press the clay gently but firmly onto the faceted surface of the bowl so the pattern is imprinted evenly.

2 / To form the shape, gently peel off and remove the imprinted clay from the upturned bowl. Turn the bowl over and lay the clay inside the bowl, pattern facing upwards. Carefully maneuver the clay, without disturbing the imprint, so that it sits centered and flush inside the bowl.

3 / To finish the shape, use the knife to cut cleanly through the excess clay around the top edge of the bowl, or leave as it is, if you prefer. Smooth the cut edge and any small cracks or imperfections with a wet finger.

4 / At the first signs of drying, gently peel away the clay from the glass bowl and then place it back in. This will allow air to get between the clay and the bowl. As the clay continues to dry, repeat this step regularly to allow more air in. Finally, once the clay feels dry enough to hold its new shape, remove it from the glass bowl and leave it on the cooling tray for at least one week until completely dry.

5 / Decorate the imprint using the paintbrush and acrylic paint. Once the paint is dry, spray the surface with sealant.

LIGHTING
chapter eight

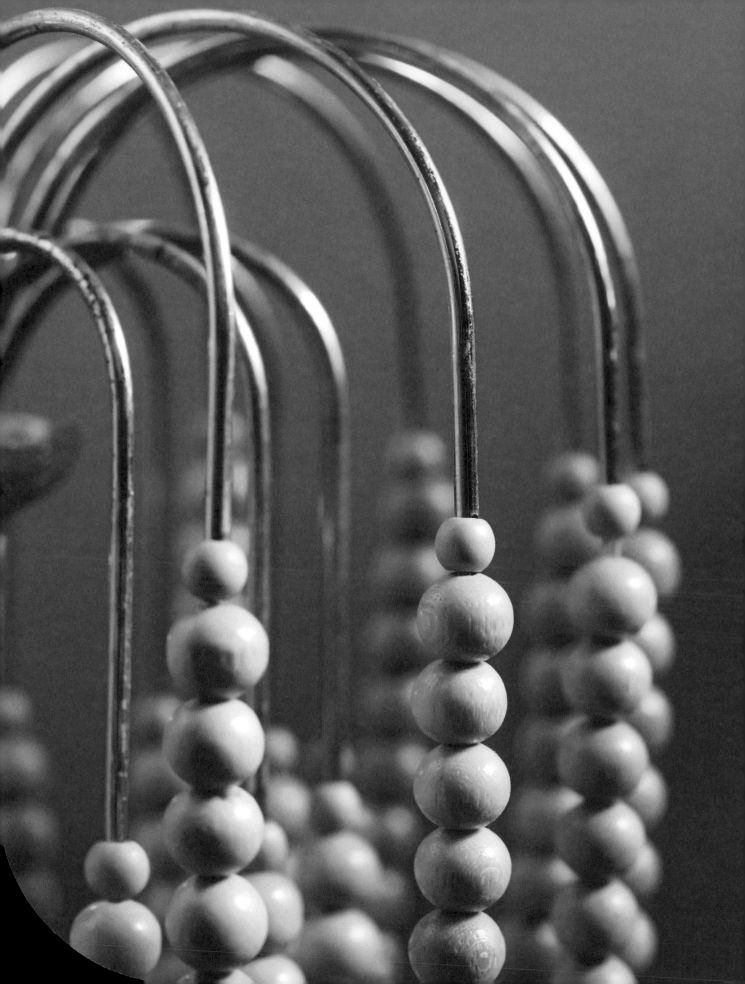

Lighting is the mood maker (or breaker if you're living with fluorescents) of every home.It is responsible for much more than just illuminating a space—it influences the ambience, which in turn affects our state of mind.

I did not realize how enthusiastic people were to explore making lighting until I designed my downloadable DIY Quilt Light template in 2011. Inspired by patchwork and supercyclers (an ever-growing international collective of designers focused on transforming perceptions of waste materials), its choice of materials and finish are left to the maker. Innovative in its approach, the template has been very successful and, in addition to being featured in many publications, it was exhibited by invitation at both London and Milan Design Weeks. Of course, there are many DIY lighting projects on the market now, so in that department we are spoiled for choice, but what about coming at lighting with a genuine maker's eye—from the aspect of making something that is one hundred percent yours, using your practice of choice?

You may not consider yourself a lighting maker, or be thinking of focusing exclusively on this aspect of a space, but whatever your practice, there is an opportunity to explore its possibilities. The following pages include the work of some wonderful makers, some of whom have ventured into lighting through further investigation of their craft and/or material. Illustrating some of the different ways lighting can be approached, these works span such outputs as ceramics, weaving, macramé, and wood turning. In my opinion, apart from the electrical and safety side of things, making lighting is perfect if you want to experience a kind of experimental practice where no rule book exists. Lighting really is the modern maker's domain and your space has the potential to be all the more distinctive for it.

"I COME ACROSS A LOT OF VINTAGE LIGHTING THAT I LOVE. REWORKING PREVIOUSLY GLITZY CRYSTAL CHANDELIERS WITH UNEXPECTED MATERIALS, SUCH AS SIMPLE WOOD BEADS, ADDS A NEW CHAPTER TO THEIR STORY AND FORMS A SPECIAL BOND BETWEEN US IN THE PROCESS."

TAMARA MAYNES

Reworked vintage brass chandelier strung with turned wood beads

"OUR WOOD LAMPS ARE HAND-TURNED AND PAINTED; EACH ONE IS
INDIVIDUAL. MAKING LIGHTING IS VERY ENJOYABLE: I LOVE CREATING
AMBIENCE AND WARM, COMFORTING ENVIRONMENTS."

BEC DOWIE & DOUGLAS SNELLING, FURNITURE & LIGHTING DESIGNERS & MAKERS
(AUCKLAND, NEW ZEALAND)

Hand-turned kauri wood lamp, hand-painted and finished with wax.

"I love that the options offered by weaving seem endless, allowing me to draw on outside inspiration. It can lead to exploration of other areas, such as lighting, to create something unique."

**KATE FARRELL, STYLIST & MOONLIGHTING WEAVER
(MELBOURNE, AUSTRALIA)**

*Steel lightshade frame wrapped in cotton yarn
and finished with tassel detail*

Q&A

Maker to Maker with...
Moya Delany, lighting designer & maker

(Melbourne, Australia)

TM: Moya, every shade you make is unique. Describe this piece.
MD: When I make a shade it is a one-off work of art. This bell shade is made from cargo parachute and Japanese kimono silk and is hand-stitched and stretched over a hand-bound frame. I have a friend who is a genius metalworker and makes all my custom frames.

TM: Some might imagine there's only so much that can be done with lighting. What's your secret to keeping your output so unique?
MD. Discovering new materials, designing new shapes, and evolving is what inspires me.

TM: Your output spans many media. How did you get into lighting?
MD: Studying Fine Art and majoring in sculpture introduced me to working across all media, so when I was approached by an interior designer about lighting work it was an easy step.

TM: What do you think lighting brings to a space?
MD: Lighting brings life to a space.

TM: Where do you make?
MD: I make mainly at home, sometimes on site when the size requires and I also take projects with me on beach holidays.

TM: So, it's safe to say you love making?
MD: Making things is the major focus of my life. If I'm not creating, then I'm not at my happiest. When I make a beautiful thing there is no greater satisfaction.

TM: Any advice for aspiring makers?
MD: Be prepared for blood, sweat, tears... and joy!

"I LOVED MAKING JEWELRY
AS A CHILD, THREADING
BEADS ONTO STRING TO MAKE
NECKLACES. IN THE SAME WAY,
MY TURNED SUSTAINABLE
WOOD BEADS ARE DESIGNED
TO BE ASSEMBLED OVER
THE HUMBLE LIGHTING CORD,
SIMILAR TO A NECKLACE."

**COCO REYNOLDS, LIGHTING & FURNITURE DESIGNER
(SYDNEY, AUSTRALIA)**

*Turned wood pendant lights
using oak, walnut, ash, and maple*

"

Rope is such a basic material. I love that I can manipulate it via a series of rudimentary knots to create something unexpected, incredibly beautiful, and seemingly intricate.

"

TAMARA MAYNES

Macramé lighting cord made with polypropylene rope

"WE STARTED COLLABORATING WHEN OUR STUDIO SPACES MERGED AND IDEAS BEGAN TO BOUNCE. WHEN WE MAKE, WE FOCUS ON BALANCE NOT SYMMETRY AND BRINGING INTERESTING SHADOW PLAY, MOODY ILLUMINATION, AND WABI-SABI BEAUTY TO A SPACE."

HARRIET GOODALL & NATALIE MILLER,
COLLABORATING FIBER ARTISTS (ROBERTSON, AUSTRALIA)

Glazed clay pendant light with woven paper cord shade

"MAKING A PROTOTYPE AND THEN RESOLVING
THE DESIGN IS THE BEST PART FOR ME.
IT'S ALL ABOUT THE PROCESS."

**COCO REYNOLDS, LIGHTING & FURNITURE DESIGNER
(SYDNEY, AUSTRALIA)**

"WE FIND IT BEST TO DESIGN BASED ON
INTUITION. IT'S IMPORTANT TO LOOK TO
THE GREAT DESIGNERS FOR INSPIRATION,
BUT IT HELPS TO NOT BE OVERLY INFLUENCED
BY ANY SPECIFIC ONE."

**STEVE NASKER & CHARLOTTE STONE, FURNITURE DESIGNERS & MAKERS
(LOS ANGELES, USA)**

"MAKING AND DESIGNING SHOULD BE
INEXTRICABLE. THE ONE SHOULD INFORM THE
OTHER IN A RECIPROCAL FEEDBACK LOOP. I LIKE
TO MOVE FREELY BETWEEN THE COMPUTER
SCREEN AND MY WORKSHOP; MY COMPUTER IS
OFTEN FOUND BALANCING PRECARIOUSLY ON MY
SLIDING TABLE SAW – I THINK THAT IMAGE SUMS
UP MY DESIGN APPROACH AND PHILOSOPHY."

**ADAM MARKOWITZ, FURNITURE DESIGNER & MAKER
(MELBOURNE, AUSTRALIA)**

a word on...
DESIGN

When a maker discovers design or vice versa, that's when real magic happens. Without design, the maker's output is void of vision and full of gaps. The process of designing something before it is made allows the maker to establish intention, tailor aesthetics, and troubleshoot functionality. Without making, the designer's output is based on an inexperienced understanding of materials and technique that will always challenge authenticity. In the past, designers were designers and makers were makers: both had a distinctive role and relied on the other in order to practice their craft. Today, however, it's a different story and the designer/maker is on a roll. With the power to see a piece through from its sketchbook conception to a beautifully crafted physical form, understanding and including the foundations of good design is the only way to immerse yourself in the complete making experience.

PROJECT N°5
woodworked light box

The template on the following pages is a guide only and not to scale. A complete ready-to-print template and layout guide can be found at www.tamaramaynes.com.

This is a simple yet super-effective lighting project for the aspiring woodworker: a versatile light that can be used on the floor or table, or hung on the wall. The technique used to form the lightweight pine box is a simple reinforced butt joint frame with countersunk screws (meaning they sit flush with the pine surface) and glued MDF face. Drilled into the face is a circular pattern of holes through which string lights protrude. The technique, along with the materials, is deliberately basic to ensure the maker is able to craft a quality, affordable light. All tools and materials can be found at large hardware stores, except the template, which will need to be downloaded online and printed out at home or an office supply store.

For cutting the pine, a table or band saw is best, although a circular saw or jigsaw will also do the job if you use a cutting guide. Failing that, you can have the pine and MDF cut where you buy them, but this will detract from your overall woodworking experience.

It's important to consider safety when working with power tools such as drills and saws, so for this project be sure to follow all manufacturers' instructions and requirements and wear protective glasses. It is also important to wear a dust mask when cutting, drilling, or sanding MDF. I also highly recommend you read and follow the manufacturer's instructions for the string-lighting component and, as always, once lighting is made and in operation, do not leave it unattended while lit.

MATERIALS

› Printed template online:
  www.tamaramaynes.com
› Masking tape
› ⅛ in (3 mm) thick MDF sheet
› 5½ in (140 mm) wide x ¾ in
  (18 mm) thick dressed pine length
  no shorter than 70 in (1.8 m)
› Sandpaper with fine grit
› Wood glue
› 1¼ in (30 mm) 8-gauge Phillips
  head wood screws
› Wood putty filler
› Spray-on undercoat
› Matte white spray paint
› 100-bulb strand of white LED
  or incandescent string lighting

TOOLS

› Pencil
› Paper scissors
› 24 in (60 cm) steel ruler
› Stanley knife & cutting mat
› Dust mask & protective glasses
› Table saw (or jigsaw if more accessible)
› Combination square
› Drill & 8-gauge wood drill/countersink bit
› Drill bit to match globe size
› Phillips head driver bit
› Band clamp & 8 in (20 cm) clamps
› Cloth & painting drop cloth
› Wood offcuts

PREPARE

1 / To prepare template, download and print out onto plain 22 x 34 in poster paper at 100%. Ensure the printed circle measures 14 in (35 cm) diameter before cutting out the template.

2 / To prepare the MDF face, mark out an 18 in (450 mm) square in pencil. Place the MDF on the cutting mat and cut out square with the Stanley knife, using the steel ruler as a cutting guide. Lightly sand cut edges.

3 / To prepare pine pieces for frame, measure and mark out two 18 in (450 mm) lengths for the top and bottom and two 16 in (414 mm) lengths for the left and right sides. Cut with a table saw (or any available saw suited to making accurate crosscuts—cuts that go across the grain of the wood). Lightly sand cut edges.

MAKE

1 / To make the pine frame, place the four cut pieces up on their sides and butt the left and right side pieces between the top and bottom pieces to form a square. Place wood glue between the corner joins, using the combination square to check that they are at exact right angles before securing with the band clamp while the adhesive sets.

2 / To secure joins, remove band clamp and measure and mark out eight screw points, as indicated on layout guide. Attach a drill/countersink bit to the drill

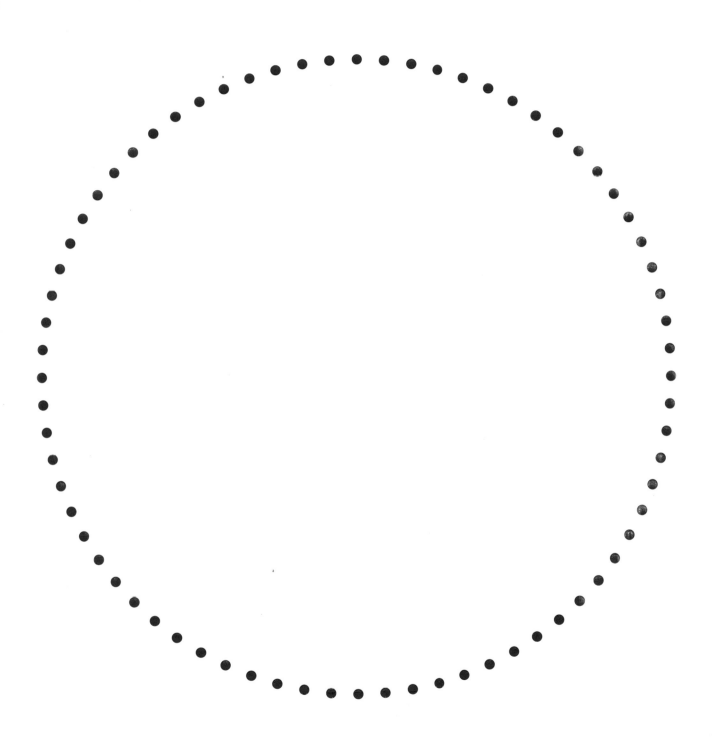

and make pilot (starter) and countersunk (a recessed area for the head of the screw to sit in) holes at marked points. Replace the drill/countersink bit with the Phillips head driver bit. Drive a screw into each of the drill holes.

3 / To attach MDF face to the pine frame, lay it face down, spread adhesive around its perimeter, and sit the pine frame on top. Ensuring all sides and corners of face and frame line up exactly, use the 8 in (20 cm) clamps to secure the top, bottom, and side joins while the adhesive sets.

4 / To transfer template to MDF face, lay template on top of face, smooth down, and, when perfectly aligned, secure around perimeter with masking tape.

5 / To drill circular pattern of holes into the MDF face, remove driver bit from drill and replace with a drill bit that matches the size of the globes on the string of lights. Next, with the box lying flat, supported underneath, and with the template-covered face up, drill holes into every point around the circle, as marked on the template. Remove the template when finished.

6 / To prepare the box for painting, fill in the small areas in recess between the screw heads and pine surface with putty filler to conceal the screws. Leave to set. Lightly sand the drill holes on both front and back of face and over the dry putty, where necessary. Wipe down entire box with a damp cloth.

7 / To paint box, lay out drop cloth, put down some wood offcuts, bricks, or even tin cans, and sit box on these to raise it slightly. Undercoat according to manufacturer's instructions and, once ready, paint matte white top coat. Leave to dry completely.

8 / To install lighting component, guide individual globes gently through drill holes from the back of the face until every hole is filled. Bundle together and tie remaining loose globes, sitting them inside the box at the back.

FURNITURE
chapter nine

My first attempt at making furniture was, in my fourteen-year-old eyes, a roaring success. A fairly crude, low-lying, open-faced wood cabinet, complete with bent nails exposing themselves where they shouldn't, it was built to house my turntable and records. This creation was my pride and joy and marked the completion of my self-initiated and executed bedroom makeover. For hours at night I sat cross-legged in front of my cabinet, playing records and memorizing lyrics, while reveling in the delight of knowing that I had built this, ahem, "fine" marriage of form and function.

Thankfully, my skills have developed since then, but further cabinets have been pushed aside in order to put my furniture-making energy into reworking many a vintage chair, rather than building from scratch. Some side-of-the-road finds, others bought for a song or inherited, what all these chairs have in common is foundations that could be transformed into something special, as determined by my analyzing maker's eye. New upholstery, a different wood stain, added decorative detail, or a complete restoration—making vintage furniture new again is something I can never seem to get enough of. It's another addiction I'm guilty of, and in no hurry to break.

The makers who have shared their furniture in the following pages are all making from feeling and that shows in their output. All adept at their chosen craft, from various woodworking techniques to upholstery and willow bending, they produce inspiring and considered work. Two in particular share my enjoyment in reworking vintage, while others' understanding of design and skill with their materials is something aspiring makers can look to achieve. While objects make up the finishing touches in a home, furniture comprises the footing, and making it takes dedication, craftsmanship, and vision. What you will have in return is a space that conveys these marvelous, enviable qualities and a feeling of accomplishment like no other.

"WHEN I MAKE I GET TO CONJURE SOMETHING NEW INTO MY WORLD. I AM ABLE TO CREATE OBJECTS THAT DIDN'T PREVIOUSLY EXIST AND THAT'S A VERY POWERFUL AND ADDICTIVE FEELING."

BRODIE VERA WOOD, FURNITURE & OBJECT MAKER (MELBOURNE, AUSTRALIA)

Geometric coffee table, using plywood and tinted varnish

Making with simple and inexpensive materials, such as plywood, has proved to me that you don't need to spend much money to make something beautiful and luxurious. Just having the feeling of what you want the work to emanate often dictates where you end up.

**BRODIE VERA WOOD, FURNITURE & OBJECT MAKER
(MELBOURNE, AUSTRALIA)**

Plywood and pine side table finished with tinted varnish

"*There is an immediate satisfaction in working with raw wood—when you see a tree become a piece of furniture. Working with milled materials isn't the same because you can already see the potential in a square-cut piece of wood.*"

GREG HATTON, FURNITURE MAKER (NEWSTEAD, AUSTRALIA)

Chainsaw-carved hardwood stool

Slatted, swivel-back hardwood chair finished with water-based paint / Daniel Barbera

"

Working with wood can be like playing music: its resonance when being worked allows you to realize that each piece is totally unique.

"

DANIEL BARBERA, FURNITURE DESIGNER & MAKER
(MELBOURNE, AUSTRALIA)

> "BEAUTIFUL WELL-DESIGNED
> WILLOW FURNITURE BRINGS
> CALMNESS TO A SPACE."

**GREG HATTON, FURNITURE MAKER
(NEWSTEAD, AUSTRALIA)**

Armchair of bent riverside willow

"I mix traditional woodcraft with contemporary digital design and fabrication. I am always surprised by what my hands discover as they work. In furniture making it is often said that your hands can feel far more than your eyes can see."

ADAM MARKOWITZ, FURNITURE DESIGNER & MAKER (MELBOURNE, AUSTRALIA)

Cantilevered chair made using laser-cut and traditionally laminated birch plywood

Q&A

Maker to Maker with...

Suzie Stanford, designer & maker of upcycled furniture & lighting

(Melbourne, Australia)

TM: Suzie, describe your unique furniture.
SS: This piece is a one-off reworked armchair using patchworked tapestry.

TM: What's the prevailing attribute of your furniture?
SS: I use discarded materials and rework them into new, more valued ones—and it's in the privilege of working with these materials that I find inspiration.

TM: This must make your process an involved one?
SS: Ideas for pieces come to me quickly, but resolving them can lead me on very different journeys. To source the many pieces I rework, I travel overseas twice a year. It starts with the shape of the furniture and story I want to tell; I will then go through hundreds of tapestries before the patchworking process and real labor

of love begins. As each tapestry has to be fitted to size, I am tatting at every moment: at the traffic lights, before breakfast, whenever I get a spare minute.

TM: What's going on in your head when you make your pieces?
SS: I celebrate previous craftsmanship and daydream of stories past told, and ones to be lived once the piece takes on a new form.

TM: What do you think reworked furniture brings to a space?
SS: Life.

TM: Any advice for aspiring makers?
SS: Follow your dreams and put your energies into creating.

"

My father, Douglas, and I started making together when I was a fine art student. A former farmer and builder, he never professes to know everything; in fact, he says he is still learning at 70.

"

BEC DOWIE & DOUGLAS SNELLING, FURNITURE & LIGHTING DESIGNERS & MAKERS
(AUCKLAND, NEW ZEALAND)

*Hand-picked and laminated
solid wood bedhead, using American
ash / Bec Dowie & Douglas Snelling*

"Working with texture is incredibly inspiring. We put both our skills on the table and they just blend so easily. When we collaborate it feels like things are in perfect alignment."

JACQUELINE FINK & LARA HUTTON, COLLABORATIVE MAKERS
SYDNEY, AUSTRALIA

Vintage stool reworked with large-scale knitted seat in felted merino wool

"I REWORK EXISTING FURNITURE MOSTLY FOR FUN AND ALSO FOR THE FACT THAT I FIND IT WASTEFUL THAT FURNITURE AND MATERIALS ARE ABANDONED WHEN, WITH A BIT OF IMAGINATION, THEY CAN BE REINVENTED AND LOVED AGAIN."

NINA TOLSTRUP, FURNITURE DESIGNER & MAKER
(STOCKHOLM, SWEDEN / LONDON, UK)

"I DON'T THINK I REALLY MAKE ANYTHING NEW; I JUST MAKE NEW CONNECTIONS. FOR ME, THE REAL ESSENCE OF MAKING WITH RECYCLED ITEMS IS REINTERPRETING THEM SO THE QUALITIES THAT MADE THEM DESIRABLE ORIGINALLY CAN BE APPRECIATED AGAIN."

SUZIE STANFORD, DESIGNER & MAKER OF UPCYCLED FURNITURE & LIGHTING
(MELBOURNE, AUSTRALIA)

"THE CHALLENGES INVOLVED IN RESTORING FURNITURE ARE VARIED. YOU ARE ALWAYS FACED WITH A VARIETY OF WEAR AND DAMAGE, EACH REQUIRING A DIFFERENT SOLUTION. WHAT I ENJOY MOST ABOUT THE PROCESS IS SEEING THE PIECE I'M WORKING ON REBIRTHED; BRINGING SOMETHING NEGLECTED BACK TO LIFE, MAKING IT SING SO IT CAN BE APPRECIATED AND LOVED ONCE AGAIN."

ADAM STEWART, RESTORER OF MID-CENTURY FURNITURE
(SYDNEY, AUSTRALIA)

a word on...
REWORKING

Innovation happens when makers focus on reworking existing furniture. This practice allows the maker endless and incredibly unique possibilities: it has everything to do with boundaries. For example, the confines set by a discarded or vintage chair frame will put the maker in a position where they need to be at their most creative, often resulting in the initial hindrances becoming the hero of the finished piece. Sourcing the material elements requires an open mind and a developed maker's eye, and involves skill and patience to edit, clean, unwork, and restore before the piece can even be formed. This aspect should be seen as just another layer of the making process: one that can help form more of a creative connection to the materials. The freedom of making from scratch is like nothing else, but with freedom can come complacency. Reworking existing pieces is not to be taken lightly... it's inspired stuff

PROJECT Nº 6
marquetry table top

The template on the following pages is a guide only and not to scale. A ready-to-print template and cutting guide can be found at www.tamaramaynes.com.

This project reworks a table to form a new top, using the concepts behind both parquetry and marquetry. Both are old decorative woodwork techniques: parquetry focuses on arranging blocks of wood into a geometric pattern and is often seen in flooring or table tops; marquetry uses thin wood veneer sheets to create finer, more intricate, and rounded designs that are attached directly to the surface of a furniture base. As this project doesn't specify veneer, rather a selection of materials closer in reference to wood blocks, and is predominantly geometric, the construction will be based on parquetry. It does, however, also rely on the "window method" used in marquetry to ensure all the cut pieces fit perfectly. Once the parquetry pattern has been formed and adhered to the MDF base, the new table top is inlayed into the table base so that the surface sits flush.

When sourcing a square table (to fit the template), choose one such as this metal cube which, once its existing top is removed, leaves a recess to inlay the new table top with either a hidden lip or brackets underneath to support it. The contrasting materials used will also need to be well thought out and all of the same thickness (I recommend ⅛ in/3 mm) in order to form a flush surface. The thickness of the MDF sheet PLUS the thickness of the pattern materials will need to equal the thickness of the recess in the top of the table. When you buy your pattern materials, ask advice on appropriate adhesives and sealants. You can rework any piece of furniture with a recess and a flat surface using this concept.

MATERIALS

› Printed template online at www. tamaramaynes.com (resized to fit)
› Large sheet of carbon transfer paper
› Large steel square, or table base
› MDF sheet, cut to size of recess in table top
› Masking tape
› Cork sheet, stiff leather, and plywood cut to size of recess in table top
› Sandpaper with fine grit
› Spray-on primer and white matte top coat
› Matte sealants for raw ply and painted ply, cork, and leather
› PVA glue or recommended adhesive

TOOLS

› Pencil
› Jigsaw
› Band saw
› Steel ruler
› X-Acto craft knife
› Dust mask & protective glasses (for wood cutting)

PREPARE

1 / To prepare template, resize to match the existing top of your table and print onto paper. Cut out around template perimeter.
2 / Use appropriate tools to remove existing top from table.
3 / To prepare new table top base, measure and mark the existing table top size onto the MDF sheet in pencil. Cut out the MDF base with the band saw.
4 / To prepare cork and leather starter pieces, measure and mark the existing table top size onto the cork and leather in pencil. Cut out with X-Acto knife.
5 / To prepare plywood starter piece, measure and mark existing table top size onto the plywood in pencil, then cut out plywood with band saw. Lay carbon paper face-down on the ply surface, followed by template face-up. Tape down to secure. Using a ruler, trace over entire pattern, except piece 10, with a pencil. Remove template and carbon paper leaving pattern on surface of the plywood.
6 / Lay MDF base and all three starter pieces alongside on your work bench.

MAKE

1 / To make parquetry pieces using the window method, separate ply sections A, B, and C with the band saw. Cut out and remove pattern piece 4 from section B. Place section C and the two remaining parts of section B on top of the cork starter piece so they are perfectly aligned. Tape ply section and parts to cork along edges and where ply edges meet. Run X-Acto knife along the "windows" (inside perimeters) of the two empty areas on the cork, to score. Remove ply and cut through cork where scored.

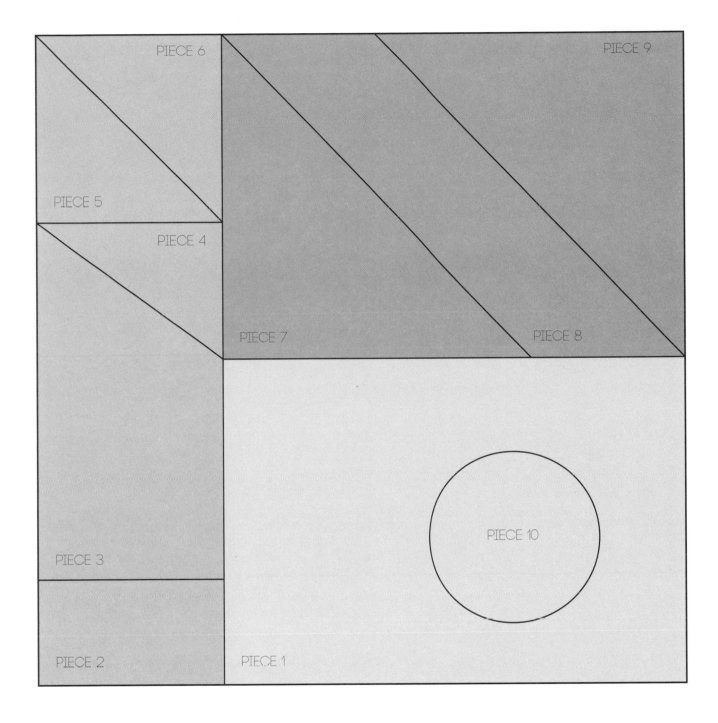

PIECE 6

PIECE 5

PIECE 4

PIECE 9

PIECE 7

PIECE 8

PIECE 3

PIECE 10

PIECE 2

PIECE 1

 SECTION A
SECTION B
SECTION C

2 / Separate ply pattern pieces 2 and 3, 5 and 6, and 7, 8, and 9 with the band saw. Place section A and ply pattern pieces 3, 4, 5, 7, and 9 on top of the leather starter piece so they are aligned. Tape ply section and pattern pieces to leather along edges and joins and where ply edges meet. Use X-Acto knife to score along windows/inside perimeters of the three empty areas on leather. Remove ply and cut leather where scored.

3 / Lay carbon paper, face-down, followed by the template, face-up, onto cork pattern piece 1. Match template to pattern piece and tape down to secure. Trace around circular pattern piece 10 with a pencil. Remove template and carbon paper, leaving pattern marked on cork. Cut out and remove pattern piece 10 from cork using the X-Acto knife.

4 / Place cork pattern piece 1 on top of ply section A so it is perfectly aligned. Tape cork pattern piece to ply section along edges with masking tape. Run pencil around window/inside perimeter of the empty area on ply to mark. Remove cork and cut out ply with jigsaw where marked.

5 / To finish ply parquetry pieces 3, 5, and 10, lightly sand the cut ply faces and edges. Place ply parquetry pieces 7 and 9 on a drop sheet, then prime and spray paint white. When dry, apply recommended matte sealant to all ply pieces.

6 / Apply matte sealants to cork parquetry pieces 1 and 4 and leather parquetry pieces 2, 6, and 8.

7 / To join finished parquetry pieces to MDF base, lay all pieces on top of MDF to ensure they fit perfectly. Stick cork parquetry piece 1 to the MDF with recommended adhesive. Butt leather parquetry piece 2 up against cork parquetry piece 1 and stick to both MDF and along the join edge with the cork, being sure not to let any glue show. Repeat for all pieces.

8 / To finish table, fit new parquetry top into existing recess and secure to supporting lip or brackets as per original table top.

MATERIALS × TOOLS
chapter ten

the maker's materials

BRASS

Brass is a metal alloy made from a combination of predominantly copper and some zinc. Strong, but not as hard as steel, it has good malleability so can be easily shaped. Brass can vary in color depending on the percentage of zinc used, and can be polished or blackened for the finished aesthetic. Like many metals used in making, brass stock is available in different forms, such as sheets, rods, wire, and pipes. However, unlike many metals, the wonderful thing about brass is that close to ninety percent is recycled, so it gets the sustainability stamp of approval.

CANE

Processed from the pithy core of a tropical climbing jungle palm called rattan, core (rattan) cane is a pliable wood-like material available in many sizes; it is popular in the weaving of baskets and lighting. In preparation for weaving, core cane must first be soaked in cold water, then wiped dry and worked between the fingers to make it supple enough to prevent splitting during use. The outer bark of the rattan that is peeled away is called chair cane and is one of the materials used to weave chair seats.

CLAY

Clay bodies—the term used for ceramic forming clays—are a mixture of natural clay and other ingredients designed to produce particular attributes, much like metal alloys. Two of the most common clay bodies are stoneware and porcelain. Stoneware, which produces an aesthetically stone-like ceramic with a dense, gritty texture, is an opaque gray/brown and has a plasticity (flexibility) that makes it perfect for use on the potter's wheel. It is tough and forgiving during forming and firing in the kiln. Porcelain, a very smooth white clay body, is particularly difficult to form on a wheel but, despite its fragility during firing and somewhat translucent aesthetic, it produces a surprisingly strong finished form.

COMPONENTS

Components are often overlooked as a material but, depending on the practice, can add further unique touches to your output. For example, when making lighting it's likely the materials required will include the actual electrical component, while furniture pieces may comprise visible hardware such as metal-worked knobs or legs. Established makers might extend their practice into producing these components, but for the aspiring maker this is rarely possible. Affording this aspect as much respect as your other materials and spending time sourcing components that will add individuality to your output is highly recommended.

DYE, PAINT, & GLAZE

Surface decoration is a technique employed both as part of practices such as ceramics or woodwork, and as the core practice itself, as in textiles. Dye, paint, and glaze are some of the most common materials used to achieve this and are suited to specific practices and substrates. Dyes, produced from natural and synthetic sources, form a chemical bond with the fiber they are coloring without altering its feel, while paint, once applied, coats the fiber's top layer, converting it into a solid film. Glazes, fused to ceramics during the firing process, are used not only for decoration but also to achieve strength and impermeability to liquids.

EXISTING MATERIALS

When it comes to a making practice based on the reworking of vintage or discarded pieces such as furniture or lighting, the materials used are predominantly existing. So, rather than sourcing new wood to construct a chair frame, the existing chair frame becomes your raw material. Alongside the endless possibilities for creativity this offers, every material has its drawbacks and those associated with existing materials are individual in that they often require unusual and lengthy preparation, such as editing, cleaning, unworking, and restoring.

the maker's materials

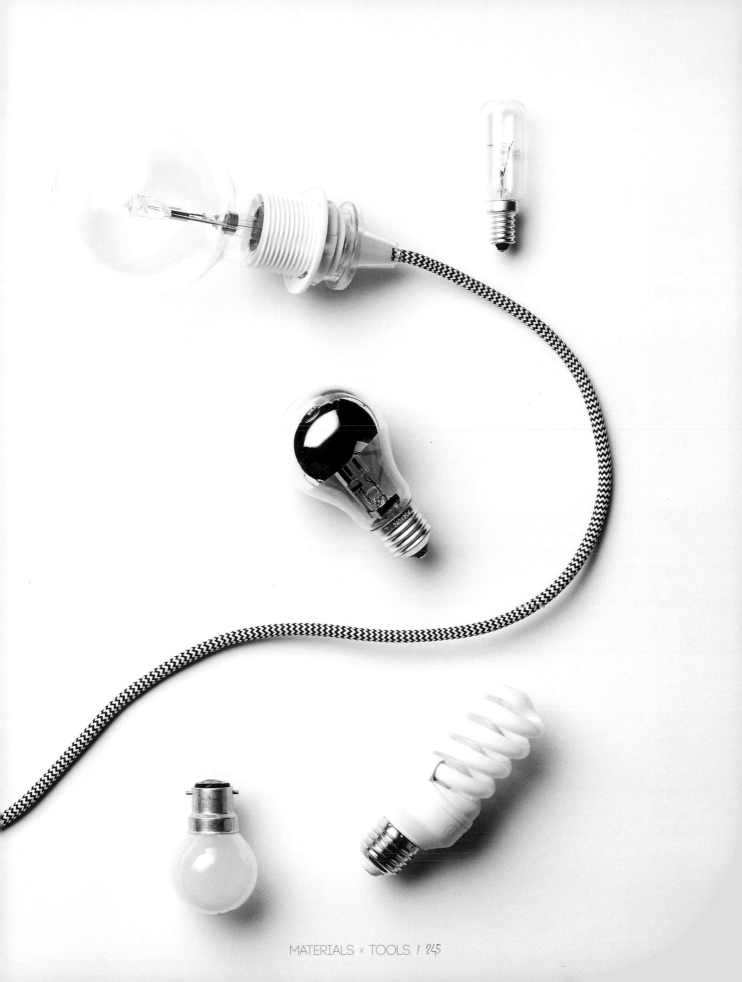

FABRIC

Most fabric is formed by the weaving of yarns on an industrial loom and is the core material for many textile practices that focus on surface decoration, such as appliqué and dyeing. Made from any of the yarn sources mentioned on page 252, the fabric weaving process, which produces cloths from durable linens to delicate silk velvets, is not to be confused with tapestry (decorative) weaving. Other types of fabric are produced by the bonding together of fibers (as in felt, which is termed "non-woven") or the interlocking of yarns (as in lace).

GLASS

If science isn't a strong point, understanding glass can be tricky for the aspiring artist to wrap their head around. Basically something wild happens to sand when it is melted at incredibly high temperatures and, no matter how much you cool it down afterwards, it will never again become truly solid. Referred to as an amorphous solid, glass is made when sand is mixed with soda ash (sodium carbonate) and limestone. Called soda-lime-silica glass, this is the most common type of glass used in forming pieces. It can be colored by the addition of metallic compounds while it is molten (in liquid form).

HARDWOOD

Used in furniture making and woodworking, hardwood originates from deciduous trees (and softwood from evergreens). You might assume that all hardwood is hard and all softwood soft, but their classifications have nothing to do with density and everything to do with botany and how trees reproduce. Having said that, most hardwoods do happen to be denser and so, along with a beautiful variety of color, texture, and grain patterns such as those found in teak and walnut, they are perfect for making long-lasting pieces that are resistant to damage. Some of the more popular hardwoods, such as ash and oak, are now grown and harvested sustainably.

LEATHER

Leather is the skin of an animal (usually cow, sheep, or goat) that has been processed to make it more durable, less inclined to deteriorate, and suitable for shaping and decorating. The process is called tanning and it involves many preparations to the skin beforehand, such as curing with salt to prevent bacterial growth during processing, and the use of a saturated solution of lime to remove natural grease. Tanning can be carried out with use of a naturally occurring vegetable chemical called tannin over several weeks, or by mineral tanning using chromium in under one day. Both methods produce handsome leathers suited to practices such as carving, dyeing, and boiling in order to mold (termed *cuir bouilli*).

PAPER

Wood pulp, typically made by either chemically or mechanically separating cellulose fibers from the wood, is used to produce the paper that is used in modeling and papier-mâché. The pressing process forcefully removes the water from within the pulp and, once dried, it effectively becomes paper. This process is followed by others that determine the paper's finish: "sizing" reduces the paper's ability to absorb liquid; coating and/or polishing produces a matte or gloss surface; and rollers can be used to create textures in the paper's surface.

PAPER CORD

Paper, or "Danish" cord is a staple in the making or restoration of mid-century inspired chairs and stools, and is also used in basket weaving. Made of treated brown kraft paper that is twisted into a strong three-ply rope, seats woven from paper cord are hard-wearing and comfortable. There are two types of paper cord, offering two distinct textures: "unlaced" has a loose twist, and "laced" a tighter twist. Paper cord became popular in the 1940s and the maker should be careful not to confuse it with fiber rush, which is a lesser quality, one-ply twisted rope, also used in chair making.

PLYWOOD

Plywood is a sheet material that is essentially a wood sandwich, consisting of core veneers covered by a face veneer. This engineered wood is produced by the mechanical gluing, rotating, and compressing of wood veneer plies (super-thin shaved layers of wood). As with every material, different types of ply are suitable for different applications and range from flexible plywood for curved pieces, to decorative ply, whose face veneer depends on the beauty and perfection of hardwoods.

ROPE

Rope is rope, right? Not quite. Once you start working with rope, in macramé for example, you will quickly realize which type best supports your chosen craft. Rope can be constructed from different fibers and in different ways, which then combine to offer different qualities for the maker. Common natural-fiber ropes, like cotton, aren't as slippery to work with as man-made fibers, such as polypropylene, but they also aren't as strong. Twisted rope has a tendency to partially untwist when it's being worked, while braided rope (which is less complicated to work with) isn't available in as many natural fibers.

STEEL

This metal alloy—meaning it's made by combining metals—consists predominantly of iron with a tiny percentage of carbon added to improve strength. Different types of steel can have extra metals added to enhance their various qualities in accordance with their proposed use. For example, stainless steel contains chromium and nickel, making it extremely resistant to corrosion and easy to clean. (Hello cutlery!) From a maker's point of view, standard (carbon) steel is generally a little softer and easier to shape than steel that includes other metals.

WOOD BLANKS

Preparing wood for turning on a lathe has had all the hard work removed by the availability of wood blanks. To produce blanks, logs are cut up in a process that removes the bark, the sapwood (soft outer layers), the pith (center, which is prone to splitting), and any faults, such as splits. Blanks either remain green (wet) or go through one more process to have their moisture removed in a kiln, after which they are referred to as dry. Both types have their pros and cons, but, being much softer than dry, green blanks are substantially easier to work with and result in a more successful turning experience.

WILLOW

Growing in abundance along riverbanks, willow trees produce branches that can be used for weaving and/or bending into baskets, sculpture, and furniture making. Any willow can be woven but the best varieties for makers contain a high percentage of wood in their long, flexible shoots. The strongest and most durable work is made when these types are fully dried before being soaked for pliability immediately prior to weaving. Both the thicker part of the branches (rods) and the smaller thin branches (switches) can be used, and furniture made from willow should be varnished to protect it from rain and sun.

YARN

Used in a diversity of textile practices such as knitting, rug making, and embroidery, yarn is a continuous twisted strand of natural or synthetic fibers and, like most materials, is available in a multitude of amazing variations. From rough to smooth, and super-bulky to incredibly fine, the suitability of yarn to craft has been refined over the years but continues to remain experimental. While natural fibers from animal and plant sources, such as wool and cotton, offer warmth, absorbency and elasticity, synthetic yarns made from chemical sources, such as polyester, are generally much easier to clean and care for.

BRUSHES

Used to apply paint and varnish to many materials, paintbrushes can be divided into two categories: decorators' brushes and artists' brushes. Both are available with either natural or synthetic filaments (fibers) for bristles, depending on the job in hand. Decorators' brushes with synthetic bristles give a smooth finish and are perfect for use with water-based paints as they don't swell; natural bristles are more effective with varnish. Artists' brushes for use with acrylic (water-soluble) paints almost always have synthetic bristles; these come with a selection of shaped tips to control the paint flow for detailed work.

CUTTING MAT

The self-healing cutting mat is the best tool ever and the one I personally can't imagine living without in my making practice. Designed through biological-based science, these mats reclose any cuts and scratches that are made on their surface. They are used underneath every material that requires cutting with a blade, to protect your work surface from damage and your blade from dulling. Self-healing, or soft-surface, cutting mats are thin, flexible, and available in a range of sizes and are, in my opinion, far superior to self-sealing, or hard-surface, cutting mats (which are very stiff so that the blade skims over the surface without cutting into it).

DRILL

Some making practices that focus on wall art (such as papier-mâché) will require a drill every now and again, but for woodwork and metalwork this tool will be compulsory. The modern maker's drill is a handheld power tool, fitted with metal cutting attachments called drill bits, which rotate to form a cylindrical hole. Drills have more guts when they are powered by electricity rather than a rechargeable battery pack; they can also be fitted with driver bits, enabling them to be used as powered screwdrivers—super handy.

the maker's tools

HAMMERS

Another basic tool that most makers will use at some stage in their practice, the hammer is used to deliver a sudden impact, often when driving a nail into wood. All hammers consist of a head made predominantly of steel, and a handle (or haft). The most common type is the claw hammer whose head consists of a flat side for impacting and a curved split side for extracting nails. Other useful hammer types are the "ball-peen" for metalwork, the "tack" for upholstery, and rubber mallets for delivering a softer blow to fragile materials.

HOT-GLUE GUN

A must for practices such as paper art, sculpting with balsa wood or other lightweight materials, and textile applications such as lightshades, a hot-glue gun is a super-quick and fairly durable way to join materials. Glue guns are available in low-temperature and hot-melt (high-temperature) versions and use a heating element to melt rods of plastic glue that are fed through by a trigger mechanism. Once melted, hot, tacky glue is squeezed out of the gun's nozzle and solidifies within seconds, meaning the maker must work quickly (and safely).

KNIVES

Knives come in a variety of shapes and sizes to meet the maker's needs, from precision craft tools used in papercraft, to heavy-duty utility knives for wood and metalwork. Having a selection on hand is essential. Knife blades are most often made from carbon steel because of its durability, strength, and ease of sharpening. Keeping the blades sharp and, in the case of carbon steel, free from rust and corrosion, will ensure accuracy and ease when working with appropriate materials.

the maker's tools

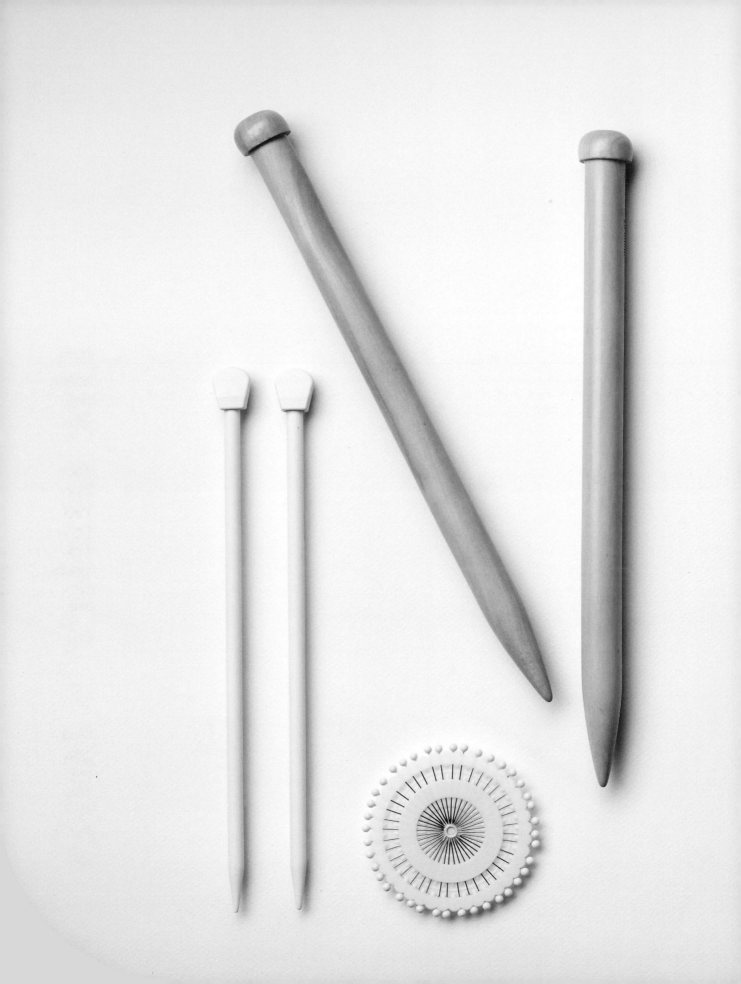

LATHE

The lathe is a motor-driven tool central to practices such as woodwork (particularly wood turning) and metalwork (for example, the spinning of metal). Wood or metal materials called workpieces are attached to the lathe via spindles (horizontal axles) at either one or both ends. The workpiece can be rotated at various speeds, allowing it to be symmetrically shaped, cut using specialized metal tools, or evenly sanded.

LOOM

Looms are used to weave fabric and tapestries by holding taut a series of vertical threads, called warp threads, while a single weft thread is interwoven across them. There are three common looms to choose from. The tapestry or frame loom has a basic rectangle frame that makes it extremely easy to warp and weave but restricts the finished tapestry to the width and length of the loom. The rigid heddle loom introduces features that create warp spacing and a shaft that adds the potential to weave lengths of cloth. Shaft looms, which can be table or floor looms, provide another level of complexity with at least four shafts operated by hand or feet levers, giving the weaver the ability to create intricate patterns and fabrics.

NEEDLES

Needles of all shapes, sizes, and materials are used for making textiles. They can be made from wood, metal, or plastic, but all are essentially long and lean with a pointed tip. Needles for sewing have an "eye" at one end through which thread is fed. Sharps are the most common and, true to their name, are very sharp. Other variations of point sharpness, eye size, length, and thickness are used for practices such as embroidery, quilting, leatherwork, and upholstery. Knitting needles have no eyes and can be very thin for fine stitches or enormously long and thick for working chunky yarns into big stitches.

the maker's tools

PINS

One of the most basic tools in the textile maker's or upholsterer's workshop is the tin of pins. Used to fasten materials together prior to permanently joining, these simple devices, made from long, thin bodies and sharp tips of steel with larger heads, are deceptively essential to many practices. With a variety of lengths and tips, pin types vary according to the material being worked.

PLIERS

Gripping, twisting, turning, bending, compressing, and cutting. . . Versatile and powerful, pliers are made up of three components: handles, jaws, and pivot, and are classified by function and the type of nose or head. One of the most useful from a making perspective are long-nose pliers, whose slender, tapered jaws come to a fine point, making them perfect for achieving precise bends in wire or holding parts too small for fingers. Other basic pliers are: flat-nose pliers, with serrated jaws for gripping, bending, and twisting; round-nose pliers, whose tapered, conical jaws are great for shaping wire loops; and cutting pliers, designed to snip through wire.

POTTER'S WHEEL

A potter's wheel is a flat, revolving disk on which wet clay is thrown (shaped) to form round ceramics. Wheels range from manual (such as the kickwheel, which is large, heavy, and propelled by foot) to electric versions, which are smaller, lighter, and often have a handy reversible rotation option. Although electric wheels have many advantages over manual—such as quicker making and less need for physical exertion —many ceramicists prefer the soothing rhythm of the manual wheel, which helps them form a stronger connection to the process than a whirring motor.

the maker's tools

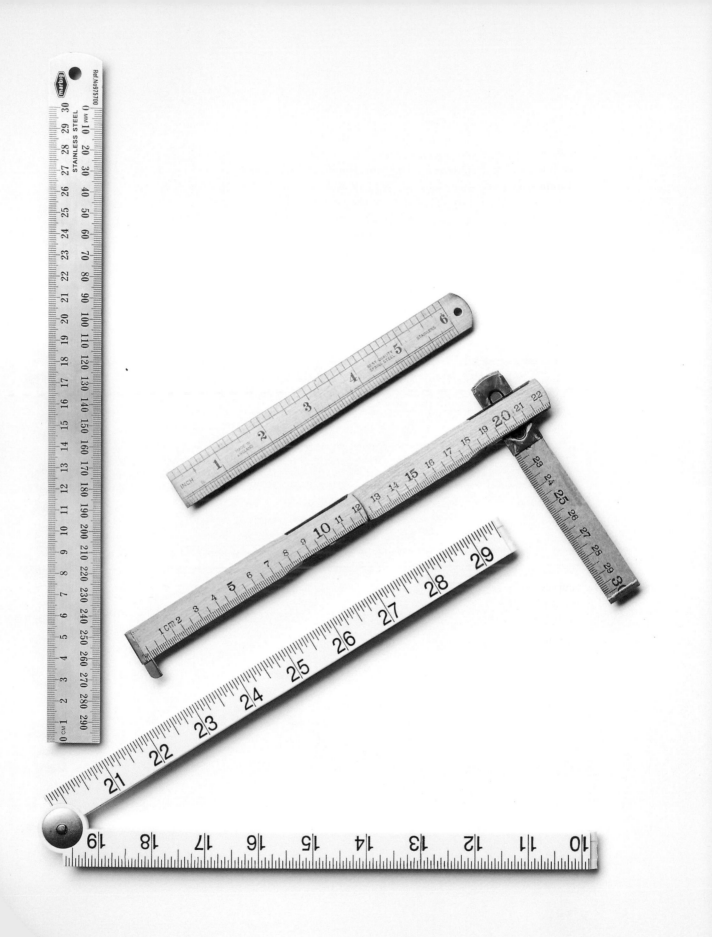

RULERS

Like scissors, rulers are a staple for most makers and, you guessed it, there is a plethora to choose from, each suited to certain practices and materials. The most common ruler length is 12 in (30 cm) and the most durable are made from metal; but rulers come in many sizes and are used not only to measure distance and rule straight lines, but also as a guide when cutting materials such as paper with a blade. Some woodworkers and other makers favor a folding ruler or retractable metal tape measure, while the ruler of choice for textiles is the tailors' tape measure, which is made from fabric or plastic for flexibility.

SANDER

Any maker who has spent time sanding their materials by hand will appreciate the speed and efficiency of a powered sanding tool. The three that will see you produce a quality output are: the orbital-finish sander, which operates in a circular motion to produce a fine, smooth finish; the belt sander, which holds a continuous loop of sandpaper and is typically used to remove material fast and aggressively, preparing the surface for the third sanding tool; and the random orbit sander, whose combination of orbital and rotary movement makes it the sander of choice for general light sanding and mark-free finishing.

SAWS

Cutting wood and metal requires a combination of hand and powered saws. Saw blades are made from steel and have teeth suited to all types of cuts and materials. For smaller work you can't go past handsaws such as the coping saw (great for cutting curves), hacksaw (for most metals), and crosscut saw (for cutting smaller pieces of wood to length). Powered saws can be handheld or stationary, with the latter giving a cleaner, more exact cut. Handhelds, such as jigsaws and circular saws, are very versatile and jigsaws can make curved as well as straight cuts. Table saws and band saws are stationary and, while the downside of a table saw is its inability to make curved cuts, it is considered the heart of any woodwork practice.

the maker's tools

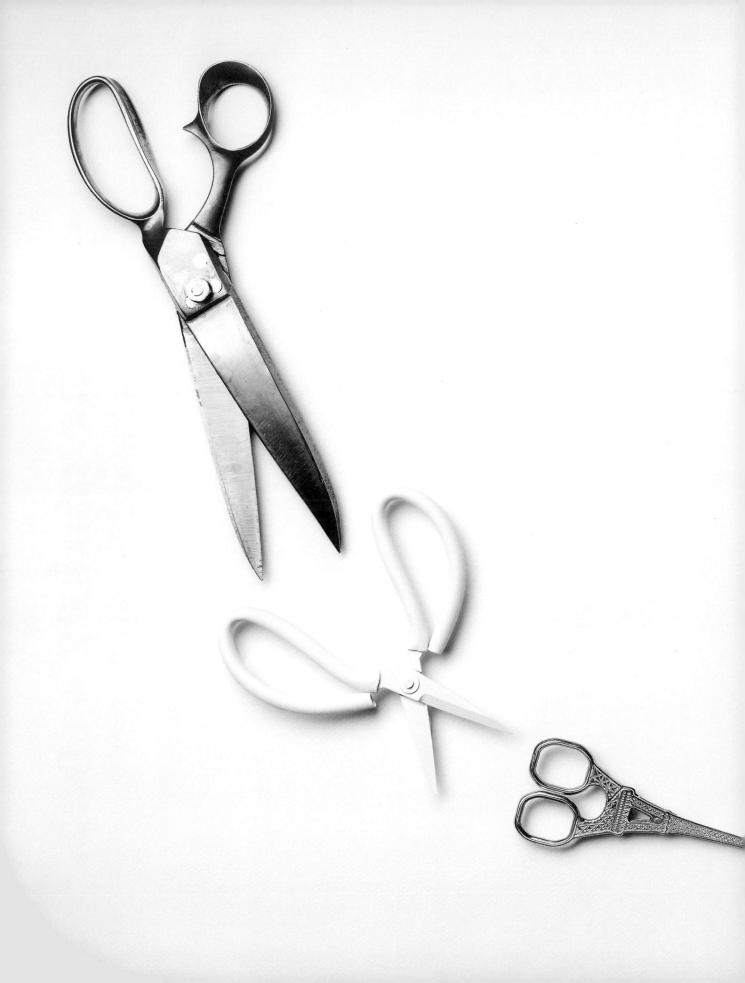

SCISSORS

Scissors, snips, shears and cutters... no matter what your craft of choice, as a maker you will use at least one pair of these in your practice. Many makers (OK, I'm referring to myself here) may look to have an unnecessarily large selection on hand, but they are all necessary for cutting different materials in different ways, I swear! Used for relatively lightweight materials, scissors are smaller than shears, which have longer blade lengths, while snips and cutters are used for metal and other dense materials.

SILKSCREEN

Designs in paint or ink can be printed onto fabric or other materials with a silkscreen. Available in many sizes, a silkscreen is essentially a rectangular wooden or aluminum frame covered in a very taut layer of silk mesh. In reality, polyester mesh is used more than silk today, but the screen is still referred to as a silkscreen. Polyester mesh comes in two forms: monofilament, which is great for exact detail and standing up to regular use; and multifilament, which prints better on textured fabrics. Silkscreens must withstand frequent washing with mild abrasives and have to be checked regularly for any pinholes that can disrupt print quality.

WELDING RIG

Using a welding rig to melt and ultimately join metals is the best option for makers practicing metalwork, who need a strong, cohesive bond that's almost as strong as the material itself. Including an electrode lead, grounding wire, and power source, the arc (stick) welding rig is one of the most basic setups. The torch welding rig, which is popular among metal sculptors and includes a welding torch and both oxygen and acetylene cylinders, is small and easy to work with. Protective clothing and a welding mask are prerequisites when using any welding rig.

who to follow...

ADAM GISTEDT
& VIKTORIA NYGREN
lisafontanarosa.com/
private/adam-viktoria/

ADAM MARKOWITZ
markowitzdesign.com

ADAM STEWART
facebook.com/Modanest

ALEXANDRA SEGRETI
& KELLY RAKOWSKI
new-friends.us

ALICIA SCARDETTA
ascardetta.com

ALISON FRASER
slabandslub.com.au

AMANDA DZIEDZIC
amandadziedzic.com.au

ANA KRAŠ
anakras.com

ANNA VARENDORFF
annavarendorff.com

ANNA-WILI HIGHFIELD
annawilihighfield.com

ANNE CARNEVALE
carnevaleclay.com

ANNEBET PHILIPS
annebetphilips.com

ARIELE ALASKO
arielealasko.com

BEC DOWIE &
DOUGLAS SNELLING
douglasandbec.com

BEN BLAKEBROUGH
blakebroughking.com

BEN MEDANSKY
benmedansky.com

BENJA HARNEY
paperform.com.au

BERN CHANDLEY
bernchandleyfurniture.
com

BRIDGET BODENHAM
bridgetbodenham.com.au

BRODIE VERA WOOD
bvw-workshop.tumblr.com

CAITLIN EMERITZ
weavinginwhite.blogspot.
com

CAROLINE SWIFT
carolineswift.com

CHRIS THORPE
headandhaft.co.uk

CHRISTIEN MEINDERTSMA
christienmeindertsma.com

CHRISTOPHER BOOTS
christopherboots.com

CLAIR CATILLAZ
clamlab.com

CLAIRE ANNE O'BRIEN
claireanneobrien.com

COCO REYNOLDS
marzdesigns.com

DANA BARNES
souledobjects.com

DANIEL BARBERA
barberadesign.com

DANIEL HULSBERGEN
studiodaniel.nl

DIANA BELTRÁN HERRERA
dianabeltranherrera.com

DION HORSTMANS
dionhorstmans.tumblr.com

DREW TYNDELL
drewtyndell.com

ELEANOR LAKELIN
eleanorlakelin.co.uk

EMILY KROLL
emily-kroll.com

ERIC TRINE
erictrine.com

FABIEN CAPPELLO
fabiencappello.com

FAYE TOOGOOD
fayetoogood.com

GARETH NEAL
garethneal.co.uk

GEMMA PATFORD LEGGE
gemmapatford.com

GEORGINA BROWN
@basic_curate

GREG HATTON
greghatton.com

HARRIET GOODALL
harrietgoodall.com

HEATHER LEVINE
heatherlevine.com

HELEN LEVI
helenlevi.com

HENRY WILSON
henrywilson.com.au

HUGH ALTSCHWAGER
www.inkstermaken.com

JACQUELINE FINK
littledandelion.com

JEM SELIG FREEMAN
AND LAURA WOODWARD
likebutter.com.au

JENNIFER STILWELL
allhandsny.com

JIN ANGDOO LEE
AND MATHIEU JULIEN
a-m-a-t-e-u-r-s.org

JOANNA FOWLES
& KATE BANAZI
lineontheside.com

JOHAN LINDSTÉN
lindstenform.com

JOHANNA DEHIO
johannadehio.de

JOSEPHINE HEILPERN
recreationcentershop.com

JOSHUA VOGEL
blackcreekmt.com

JULIE LANSOM
julielansom.com

JUSTINE ASHBEE
nativeline.com

KARA HYNES
karahynes.com

KAREN BARBÉ
karenbarbe.com

KATE FARRELL
katefarrell.com.au

KATE KEARA PELEN
katekearapelen.net

KATHERINE MAY
katherinemay.com

KATHY DALWOOD
kathydalwood.com

KELLEN TUCKER
sharktoothnyc.com

KYUHYUNG CHO
kyuhyungcho.com

LANCE & NIKOLE HERRIOTT
herriottgrace.com

LARA HUTTON
larahutton.com

LAUREN BAMFORD
laurenbamford.com

LINDSAY ROGERS
lindsayrogersceramics.com

LISA GARCIA
sonadora.co

LIVIA POLIDORO
liviapolidoro.com

LOLA LELY
lolalely.com

LUBNA CHOWDHARY
lubnachowdhary.co.uk

MAE ENGELGEER
mae-engelgeer.nl

MALINDA REICH
malindareich.com

MARI ANDREWS
mariandrews.com

MARIUSZ MALECKI
studio-ziben.de

MARSHA GOLEMAC
marshagolemac.com

MARYANNE MOODIE
maryannemoodie.com

MATTHEW & ANDREW GALVIN
galvinbrothers.co.uk

MATTHEW CLELAND
scoreandsolder.com

MAURA AMBROSE
folkfibers.com

MAX LAMB
maxlamb.org

MAY STERCHI
himoart.com

MEG CALLAHAN
megcallahan.com

MICHELE MICHAEL
elephantceramics.com

MICHELE QUAN
mquan.com

MIMI JUNG & BRIAN HUREWITZ
earlyworkstudio.com

MIRIAM AUST & SEBASTIAN AMELUNG
aust-amelung.com

MOYA DELANY
moyadelany.com

MR FINCH
mister-finch.com

NAOMI PAUL
naomipaul.co.uk

NATALIE MILLER
nataliemillerdesign.com

NATALIE WEINBERGER
natalie w.com

NICK PEARCE
nickpearce.com.au

NIGEL & RAWIA COTTERILL
ndcstore.co.nz

NINA TOLSTRUP
studiomama.com

PAGE THIRTY THREE
pagethirtythree.com

PAULA GREIF
paulagreifceramics.com

PEPA MARTIN & KAREN DAVIS
shibori.com.au

REBECCA ATWOOD
rebeccaatwood.com

RENILDE DE PEUTER
at-swim-two-birds.blogspot.com.au

RIK TEN VELDEN
riktenvelden.com

ROBERT DOUGHERTY & JANELLE PIETRZAK
allroadsdesign.com

ROMY NORTHOVER
romyno.com

SALLY ENGLAND
sallyengland.com

SARAH K
blakebroughking.com

SARAH K & LIANE ROSSLER
supercyclersarego.blogspot.com.au

SARAH PARKES
smalltown.net.au

SHARON MUIR
sharonmuir.com

SOOJIN KANG
soojinkang.net

SOPHIE WOODROW
sophiewoodrow.co.uk

STELLA BAGGOTT
atelierstella.bigcartel.com

STEPHEN ANTONSON
stephenantonson.com

STEVE NASKER & CHARLOTTE STONE
pacificwonderlandinc.com

SUPERCYCLERS
supercyclersarego.blogspot.com.au

SUZANNE SULLIVAN
thewideprospect.tumblr.com

SUZIE STANFORD
@suzannesullivanceramics

TAMAR MOGENDORFF
tamarmogendorff.com

TARA CARBONARA
@taracarbonara

TARA SHACKELL
tarashackell.com

THE FORTYNINE STUDIO
thefortynine.com.au

TORTIE HOARE
tortiehoare.co.uk

TRACEY DEEP
@floralsculptures

TRACY WILKINSON
twworkshop.com

VANESSA KNIGHT
ableground.bigcartel.com

VICTORIA PEMBERTON
bindandfold.bigcartel.com

VOICES OF INDUSTRY
voicesofindustry.com

WONA BAE
wonabae.com

YOKO OZAWA
cargocollective.com/yokoozawa

acknowledgments

THANK YOU TO THE LONG LIST OF TALENTED MAKERS
WHO CONTRIBUTED THEIR OUTPUT OR VOICE:

Adam Markowitz
Adam Stewart
Alison Fraser
Amanda Dziedzic
Anna Varendorff
Bec Dowie & Douglas Snelling
Ben Blakebrough
Benja Harney
Bern Chandley
Bridget Bodenham
Brodie Vera Wood
Coco Reynolds
Daniel Barbera
Dion Horstmans
Gemma Patford Legge
Georgina Brown
Greg Hatton

Harriet Goodall & Natalie Miller
Jacqueline Fink
Jennifer Stilwell
Joanna Fowles & Kate Banazi
Kara Hynes
Kate Farrell
Kate Keara Pelen
Kathy Dalwood
Lara Hutton
Lauren Bamford
Mae Engelgeer
Marsha Golemac
Maryanne Moodie
Maura Ambrose
Meg Callahan
Michele Michael
Michele Quan

Moya Delany
Nick Pearce
Nina Tolstrup
Pepa Martin & Karen Davis
Sally England
Sarah K
Sarah K & Liane Rossler aka
    Supercyclers
Stella Baggott
Steve Nasker & Charlotte Stone
Suzanne Sullivan
Suzie Stanford
The Fortynine Studio
Victoria Pemberton
Viktoria Nygren & Adam Gistedt
Wona Bae

EXTRA BIG THANKS TO THOSE WHO SHOWED EXTREMELY GENEROUS
SUPPORT IN THE FORM OF SPONSORSHIP:

Dulux Australia and Cristina at Communicado (paint colors used throughout) www.dulux.com.au
Virginia at The Bedouin Societe (linen bedding used throughout) www.bedouinsociete.com
The Establishment Studios (props and studio space used throughout) www.theestablishmentstudios.com.au

THANK YOU TO THOSE WHO GAVE KIND ASSISTANCE WITH PRODUCT
LOANS, PROPS, SPONSORSHIP, OR ORGANIZING THEIR OTHER HALF:

Amanda at Douglas & Bec
Anthony Basheer
Bree at Mr Kitly
Bree Leech & Heather Nette King
Christina at Design Stuff

Katie at The Family Love Tree
Katie Marx
Lydia at Matter
Lyn at Gardener & Marks
Miranda Skoczek

Petrina Turner
Rachael at Criteria Collection
Rebecca Vitartis

VERY SPECIAL THANKS GO TO:

Sascha Klave, my main squeeze, who gave up much to support me while I saw this project through. Thank you, darling boy, for putting up with my preoccupied mind, pretending to be ok spending evenings and weekends alone, allowing the past year to be all about me, and ultimately not divorcing me as a result! I appreciate it far more than I have said or shown.

My family and friends who have barely seen or heard from me in almost a year while I was all consumed. Thank you for your love, understanding, and patience.

Tracy Lines, the dear friend, ever talented book designer and publishing partner in crime whom I love immensely for really understanding me, getting this book rolling, providing endless, valuable input, and propping me up when I thought I might crumble. You, love, are beyond amazing.

Eve Wilson, the dream photographer, who not only gave up so many of her weekends to help me create images we could be proud of, but for whom nothing was ever a problem. A total star to work with, who could definitely convince me to do it all again.

Kate Farrell, the incredible styling assistant and total life saver, who worked alongside me week after week. The gestures of appreciation she has so far been shown are just the beginning of my gratitude for her six-months-plus of loyalty and meticulous help.

Bree Flack and Bronwyn Loftus, the amazing shoot assistants, who were so supportive of this project that they gave up many a weekend to paint wall flats, build sets, and generally work their butts off. You ladies rock.

Elisenda Russell and Rochelle Seator, Eve's fabulous photography assistants, whose talents extended into hand modeling and finishing my embroidery for me. Props to you, ladies.

Glen Proebstel and Rachael Hart, whose beautiful space has become my home away from home and whose incredible generosity has allowed me to spread my wings. My most heartfelt thanks for bringing me to Melbourne and unknowingly providing the perfect platform for this project.

Carly Spooner, friend, comrade, and general all-round lady of awesomeness, who helped me in so many seemingly small ways throughout this project that she deserves a humongous thank you.

Karina Sharpe, the super-clever creative, who dropped everything to lend her talent and articulate eye to this project in the form of awesome collages and perfect project templates.

Georgia Ramman, the incredibly patient hair and makeup artist, who jumped on board at the last minute to contribute her talent so beautifully.

Thanks also to photography and shoot assistants Anthony Basheer, Ellie Beauchamp, Amy Mehrten, and Naomi Burd, who graciously gave their time and talent.

Last, but certainly not least, my publisher, Murdoch Books, and the key people there who believed in this project enough to give me the incredible opportunity to make it real. Diana Hill, Jane Price, and Vivien Valk: I really cannot thank you all enough.

Editor, ABRAMS edition: Cristina Garces
Production Manager, ABRAMS edition: Kathleen Gaffney
Cover Design, ABRAMS edition: Najeebah Al-Ghadban
Publisher: Diana Hill
Designer: Tracy Lines

Library of Congress Control Number: 2016961382

ISBN: 978-1-4197-2721-4

Text copyright © 2017 Tamara Maynes
Design copyright © 2015 Murdoch Books
Photographs copyright © 2017 Eve Wilson
First published in 2015 by Murdoch Books, an imprint of Allen and Unwin

Printed and bound in China
10 9 8 7 6 5 4 3 2 1

Abrams books are available at special discounts when purchased in
quantity for premiums and promotions as well as fundraising or educational
use. Special editions can also be created to specification. For details, contact
specialsales@abramsbooks.com or the address below.

ABRAMS
The Art of Books

115 West 18th Street
New York, NY 10011
abramsbooks.com